Duden

Einfach klasse in Englisch

9. Klasse

Wissen • Üben • Testen

Dudenverlag
Mannheim • Leipzig • Wien • Zürich

Fabienne Wittig

Bibliografische Informationen der Deutschen Nationalbibliothek
Die Deutsche Nationalbibliothek verzeichnet diese Publikation in der Deutschen Nationalbibliografie; detaillierte bibliografische Daten sind im Internet über http://dnb.ddb.de abrufbar.

 D C B A

Redaktionelle Leitung Annika Renker
Redaktion Linda Strehl
Autorin Birgit Hock

Herstellung Annette Scheerer
Layout Horst Bachmann
Illustration Carmen Strzelecki
Umschlaggestaltung Sven Rauska
Umschlagabbildung Ullstein Bild, Berlin

Satz Katrin Kleinschrot, Stuttgart
Druck und Bindung Appl, Wemding
Printed in Germany

ISBN-13: 978-3-411-72591-5
ISBN-10: 3-411-72591-5

Inhaltsverzeichnis

INHALT

1 Die Zeiten

1.1 Das *present tense*

Im Englischen gibt es zwei verschiedene Möglichkeiten, gegenwärtige Handlungen oder Zustände auszudrücken: das *simple present* und das *present progressive* (auch *present continuous*).	It never rains in California. Look! It's raining.

Das *simple present*

Die Form des *simple present* entspricht dem Infinitiv des Verbs.	I **like** summer, sunshine and holidays.
Aufgepasst: In der 3. Person Singular wird immer ein *-s* angehängt!	Sarah love**s** her dog.
Das *simple present* wird verwendet, wenn etwas regelmäßig, häufig, oft, nie oder auch immer geschieht. **Signalwörter:** *always, sometimes, first, never, often, usually, every (day / week / month / year), generally.*	Father reads a story to his children every night. My grandparents never go out for dinner. We usually have toast for breakfast.
Bei **Fragen** und **verneinten Aussagen** werden die Formen *do / does* und *don't / doesn't* verwendet.	Do you listen to music often? – No, I don't. He doesn't do his homework often.

Das *present progressive*

Das *present progressive* wird gebildet mit einer konjugierten Form des Hilfsverbs *be* und der *-ing*-Form des Vollverbs.	I **am watering** the flowers. She **is waiting** for her boyfriend to arrive.
Aufgepasst: Für das *present progressive* gibt es im Deutschen keine Entsprechung. Es wird verwendet, um Tätigkeiten oder Vorgänge zu beschreiben, die im Moment des Sprechens im Gange, also noch nicht abgeschlossen sind. **Signalwörter:** *(right) now, at the moment, just, Look!, Listen!*	The sun isn't shining at the moment. Listen! They are playing my favourite song. What are you doing? – I am just writing a letter. While Tom is talking to a friend on the phone, he is drawing lines in his notebook.

ÜBUNG 1 ***Simple present*** **oder** ***present progressive?*** **Setze die richtige Zeitform des in Klammern angegebenen Verbs ein.**

After a long day at school, Laura __________ (come) home, __________ (throw) her school bag into the corner and __________ (walk) into the kitchen. Her mother __________ (cook) dinner.

Laura: "Hi, Mum! Oh, you __________ (not / prepare) potato soup again, are you?"

Mother: "Potato soup? Of course, Laura! Whenever I __________ (cook), I always __________ (cook) soup or stew *(Eintopf)*. You should __________ (know) that I can't __________ (cook) anything else."

Laura: "Oh Mum, you __________ (tease). You __________ (know) very well how much I __________ (love) your lasagne."

Mother: "Yes, I __________ (know). But lasagne __________ (be) always a lot of work, and I came home from work only fifteen minutes ago. Listen! The phone __________ (ring). Can you __________ (answer) it, please?"

Laura __________ (walk) into the living room and __________ (pick up) the phone. She __________ (still / talk) to her friend when her Dad __________ (walk) into the house.

Dad: "Hello everybody!"

Mother: "Hello, Peter. Laura __________ (be) in the living room."

Dad: "Oh Laura, you're crazy! Whenever I __________ (come) home from work, you __________ (talk) on the phone. Listen! Mother __________ (call). Dinner __________ (be) ready."

Laura __________ (say) good-bye to her friend on the phone, __________ (replace) the receiver and __________ (walk) into the kitchen. The whole family __________ (eat) dinner. But soon enough, the phone __________ (ring) again ...

WISSEN+

Verben ohne *present progressive* Folgende Verben werden üblicherweise nur im *simple present* verwendet:	
■ Verben der Sinneswahrnehmung: *to see, to taste, to feel,*	Listen! I hear somebody cry.
■ Zustandsverben: *to seem, to look, to own, to consist of, to contain, to possess, to result,*	You seem happy. You look sad. They own a big house.
■ Verben, die Einstellungen oder Gefühle ausdrücken: *to think, to forget, to mind, to agree, to believe, to doubt, to find, to mean, to imagine, to know,*	I think mother will be able to help me. He doesn't mind our being late.
■ Verben, die Wünsche oder Abneigungen formulieren: *to wish, to want, to like, to desire, to please, to prefer, to mind.*	He wants to be a doctor. I like my tea hot and strong.
Aufgepasst: Einige dieser Verben können dennoch eine *progressive*-Form bilden. Dann allerdings ändert sich ihre Bedeutung!	I'm thinking of → ich überlege / denke darüber nach she's tasting → sie probiert / versucht she's seeing (the doctor) → sie sucht (den Arzt) auf he's wanting in (good behaviour) → es fehlt ihm an (gutem Benehmen)

ÜBUNG 2 **Übersetze die Verben in den folgenden Sätzen und mache dir den Bedeutungsunterschied klar.**

a) Our teacher always forgets his book. →

I am forgetting my French. →

b) This vine tastes awful. →

She is tasting red vine with some chocolates. →

c) She wants to become a teacher. →

Their daughter is wanting in good manners. →

d) She is seeing a psychiatrist. →

He always sees his daughter on Sundays. →

e) I'm thinking of going to London. →

I think he's right. →

ÜBEN

1.2 Das *past tense*

Das *simple past*

Die regelmäßigen Formen des *simple past* werden gebildet, indem man die Endung -*ed* an den Infinitiv des Vollverbs hängt.	I **listened** to their stories. We **talked** and **laughed** all night.
Tipp: Die unregelmäßigen Formen solltest du auswendig können. Schlage in deiner Schulgrammatik nach und wiederhole sie!	to be → was to hear → heard to speak → spoke
Das *simple past* wird verwendet, um auszudrücken, dass eine Handlung oder ein Vorgang bereits abgeschlossen ist, oder um einen bestimmten Zeitpunkt in der Vergangenheit zu benennen. **Signalwörter:** *last, ago, yesterday, once, used to, in 1999*	Sarah bought a dress. We spent a week in California in August 2005 / last summer. I used to practice ballet when I was a girl.
Bei **verneinten Aussagen** und **Fragen** werden die Formen *did* und *did not / didn't* verwendet.	Sarah **didn't buy** a pair of shoes yesterday. **Did** she really **buy** a new dress yesterday?

Das *past progressive*

Das *past progressive* wird aus der *simple-past*-Form von *to be (was / were)* und der -*ing*-Form des Vollverbs gebildet.	I **was buying** we **were watching**
Das *past progressive* steht, wenn zwei Dinge bzw. Ereignisse in der Vergangenheit gleichzeitig stattgefunden haben. Es kann auch Hintergründe und Begleitumstände eines Ereignisses oder einer Handlung näher beschreiben. **Signalwörter:** *all (day / week), while*	Laura was doing her homework when the phone rang. While it was raining heavily outside, we enjoyed sitting in front of the TV. My sister was preparing cakes for her birthday party all day.
Um eine Aussage im *past progressive* zu **verneinen** oder eine **Frage** zu formulieren, wird zwischen *was / were* und die -*ing*-Form ein *not* geschoben bzw. *was / were* an den Satzanfang gestellt.	The girls were not / weren't playing chess. Were they playing football? – No, they were playing badminton.

ÜBUNG 3 **Wie gut kannst du die unregelmäßigen Verben? Fülle die Tabelle vollständig aus.**

infinitive	*simple past*	**deutsche Bedeutung**
	caught	
to lie		
	won	
		werfen
	became	
to fall		
		zeigen
to read		

ÜBUNG 4 **Was geschah zuerst? Schreibe sinnvolle Sätze und verwende jeweils die korrekte Zeitform im *simple past* oder *past progressive*.**

Sarah / read / the newspaper – the doorbell / ring

Sarah was reading the newspaper when doorbell rang.

my big sister / prepare dinner – the electricity / go off

Laura / play the violin – the telephone / ring

father / dust the cupboard – the match between Liverpool and Manchester / end

the shop assistant / try on / an expensive dress – her boss / come in

the taxi driver / park / in a handicapped parking space – the police / drive by

my friends and I / walk home – it / start to rain

ÜBUNG 5 ***Simple past*** **oder** ***past progressive?*** **Setze die richtigen Formen ein.**

Last summer, I ______ (have) a very frightening experience. At that time I ______ (travel) the United States. I used to ______ (put up) my tent quite regularly in one of the many National Parks, and I always ______ (sleep) very well. One night, however, at about 9 o'clock at night, while I ______ (read) a book by the flickering light of my torch, I ______ (hear) somebody scream. I ______ (close) my book and ______ (turn) my flashlight off. I ______ (lace up / just) my shoes when I ______ (hear) a terrible snort.
Something enormous ______ (stand) in front of my tent! I ______ (not / dare) to breath. "That might be a bear," I ______ (think). Then I ______ (remember) my whistle. I ______ (blow) the whistle and the bear ______ (disappear). I ______ (tremble / still) when I ______ (turn) my flashlight on again and I ______ (not / sleep) well that night.
Next morning, when I ______ (go) into the next village to do some shopping, I ______ (ask) a ranger *(Parkwächter)* about bears in national parks. He ______ (tell) me that there had been no bear around at all the previous night.
I ______ (tremble) again: ______ I ______ (have) a dream when I ______ (hear) the screaming and snorting last night?

ÜBUNG 6 **Übersetze die Sätze ins Englische und schreibe sie in dein Übungsheft.**

Großvater hat gestern Nachmittag drei Stunden im Garten gearbeitet.
Der Taxifahrer kannte die Stadt überhaupt nicht.
Jill saß gerade an den Hausaufgaben, als ihr Freund zu Besuch kam.
Unser Mathelehrer war heute überhaupt nicht nett.
Wo warst du, als es anfing zu schneien?

1.3 Das *present perfect*

Das *present perfect simple* und das *present perfect progressive* werden verwendet, um Handlungen oder Zustände zu beschreiben, die Vergangenheit und Gegenwart verbinden.

Das *present perfect simple*

Das *present perfect simple* bildet man aus dem Hilfsverb *has / have* und dem Partizip Perfekt *(past participle)* des Vollverbs.	I **have eaten** my sandwich. She **has dropped** her bag.
Tipp: Wiederhole die unregelmäßigen Formen des *present perfect simple!*	to write → written to go → gone
Das *present perfect simple* drückt aus, dass ein Ereignis in der Vergangenheit begonnen hat und bis in die Gegenwart hinein andauert bzw. einen Effekt in der Gegenwart hat.	I have painted my bike. It's yellow now. *(Der Effekt des Streichens ist jetzt sichtbar.)*
Signalwörter: *already, never, before, (not) yet, since, for*	I have already eaten two pieces of cake. I haven't seen Robbie Williams' new video yet.

Das *present perfect progressive*

Das *present perfect progressive* setzt sich zusammen aus *have / has been* und dem Vollverb in *-ing*-Form.	I **have been dreaming** he **has been living**
Auch das *present perfect progressive* drückt aus, dass eine Handlung oder ein Ereignis in der Vergangenheit begonnen hat und bis in die Gegenwart hinein andauert. Es betont aber die Dauer der Handlung bzw. des Ereignisses.	I have been doing my homework since 3 o'clock in the afternoon *(und bin immer noch nicht fertig damit).* He has been watching TV for four hours now *(und schaut weiterhin fern).*
Signalwörter: *how long?, all (day / week), for, since*	How long have you been watching TV?
Um Sätze im *present perfect* zu **verneinen,** wird *not* zwischen *have / has* und das Partizip Perfekt bzw. *been* + *-ing*-Form geschoben.	I have not washed my car. I have not been riding my bike recently because it's got a puncture *(Platten).*

ÜBUNG 7 **Beherrschst du die *past participle*-Formen? Fülle die Tabelle vollständig aus.**

infinitive	*past participle*	deutsche Bedeutung
to sell		
	risen	
		legen, stellen
to bite		
	grown	
to know		
		anfangen
to draw		

ÜBUNG 8 **Nur eine Antwort ist richtig – kreuze die richtige Lösung an und trage sie in die Lücken ein.**

My new dog is named Bonzo. I ______ of having a pet.

- ☐ had been dreaming ☐ always dreamt ☐ have always dreamt

It's 10 p. m. already. How long ______ TV?

- ☐ have you been watching ☐ did you watch ☐ were you watching

My parents ______ to China.

- ☐ were going ☐ have been going ☐ have never been

I'm exhausted. I ______ the house since 8 o'clock this morning.

- ☐ was cleaning ☐ have been cleaning
- ☐ cleaned

Look at this mess! I ______ my bag.

- ☐ dropped ☐ was dropping ☐ have dropped

ÜBEN

WISSEN +

since und for

Since bezeichnet den genauen Zeitpunkt, zu dem eine Handlung einsetzte. *For* bezeichnet eine Zeitspanne oder die Dauer eines Geschehens oder einer Handlung.	I have had this job since 2003. I have had this job for three years.
Since und *for* können auch mit dem *present perfect progressive* stehen.	He has been doing his homework since three o'clock. Laura has been playing the violin for six years now.

ÜBUNG 9 **Formuliere die folgenden Sätze um, indem du *for* oder *since* benutzt. Achte außerdem auf die richtige Form – *simple* oder *progressive?***

Sara and Bill live in California. They arrived there five years ago.

Sara and Bill have been living in California for five years.

Hanna plays the piano. She started it when she was six years old.

We prepare a dinner party. We started to prepare it at 4 p.m.

My dad has got an old computer. He bought it in 1990.

Amy and Evan own a house. They bought it six years ago.

Petra sends me a postcard every week. She moved here two months ago.

ÜBUNG 10 ***Present perfect simple* oder *present perfect progressive?* Achte beim Übersetzen auf die richtige Zeit im Englischen und schreibe in dein Übungsheft!**

Unsere Schule hat seit Anfang des Jahres einen neuen Direktor.
Seit Januar hat sich vieles geändert.
Wie lange suchst du schon nach deinem Ohrring?
Die Millers haben ihr altes Auto noch nicht verkauft.
Ben hat heute schon zwei Schokoladenriegel gegessen.

1.4 Das *past perfect*

Das *past perfect* beschreibt Ereignisse, die weit in der Vergangenheit zurückliegen. Es entspricht dem deutschen Plusquamperfekt.	We **had already eaten** when our friends arrived. We **had been eating** when the table collapsed.

Das *past perfect simple*

Das *past perfect simple* setzt sich zusammen aus der Form *had* und dem Partizip Perfekt *(past participle)* des Vollverbs. Es wird verwendet, um auszudrücken, dass eine Handlung in der Vergangenheit zeitlich *vor* einer anderen Handlung in der Vergangenheit stattgefunden hat (= Vorvergangenheit). **Signalwörter:** *after, when, before*	I **had listened** she **had caught** Rick had turned the TV off before his father came home from work. Tina was late for school because she had missed the bus.

Das *past perfect progressive*

Das *past perfect progressive* setzt sich zusammen aus der Form *had been* und der *-ing*-Form des Vollverbs. Es wird verwendet, um auszudrücken, dass ein Ereignis bzw. eine Handlung in der Vergangenheit noch andauerte, während ein anderes Ereignis begann.	I **had been listening** we **had been thinking** They had been watching the news when the tornado hit their area. The fans had been throwing bottles before the police arrived.
Um Sätze, die im *past perfect* stehen, zu **verneinen,** wird ein *not* zwischen *had* und das Partizip Perfekt geschoben (Kurzform: *hadn't*). In **Fragesätzen** steht entweder das Fragewort oder das Hilfsverb *had* am Satzanfang.	I had not listened to the news. The baby hadn't been crying before the babysitter arrived. Had the baby been crying before the babysitter arrived? What had the baby been doing when the babysitter arrived?
Merke: Im *past perfect* wird häufig die Kurzform *'d* anstelle von *had* verwendet.	I'd listened to the news. They'd been watching the news when the tornado hit their area.

WISSEN

ÜBUNG 11 **Lies dir die folgende Geschichte durch und markiere alle Verben. Erzähle dann die Geschichte absatzweise rückwärts, indem du das *past perfect* benutzt. Schreibe in dein Übungsheft.**

Yesterday, Evan got up early and took his kids to the zoo. Maya enjoyed watching the penguins, and Milo had a lot of fun feeding the ducks. After a picnic lunch, Evan bought the kids an ice cream. Maya and Milo were running around the zoo for many hours and had a perfect day. At home, Evan's wife Amy had a wonderful day, too. She enjoyed the quietness. She took a bath. She read a book and took a nap *(Nickerchen)* in the sunshine.
And after so many hours to herself, she was looking forward to seeing her family again.

Yesterday, after many hours to herself, Amy had been looking forward to seeing her family again. She had had a wonderful …

ÜBUNG 12 **Sarah und Sam wollen heiraten. Schreibe vollständige Sätze mit dem *past perfect simple*. Beginne jeden Satz mit *after*. Schreibe in dein Übungsheft.**

Sarah and Sam / decide to marry / send out invitation cards

they / send out invitation cards / look around for a nice party location

Sarah and Sam / decide on a meal / go shopping for a wedding dress and a suit

they / have everything ready / Sam and Sarah / panic: the idea of having such a big party was simply too much for them

they / say sorry to all their friends / the two of them / fly to the Caribbean Sea

they / get married / on the beach of a romantic island / have a wonderful honeymoon

ÜBUNG 13 **Setze die richtige Zeitform in die Lücken. Aufgepasst: Es kommen nicht nur Zeiten der Vergangenheit vor!**

Many years ago, while I ______ (live) in New Zealand, I once ______ (go) whale-watching on a small boat.

I ______ (be) to London twice already.

Sarah ______ (be) late for lunch because she ______ (miss) the school bus.

We ______ (spend) our holidays in Africa last summer.

When I ______ (be) a little girl, my sister and I ______ (quarrel) many times a day.

Kim ______ (visit) her friend in hospital twice since last Sunday.

We always ______ (have) cereal for breakfast.

Her brother came home while Laura ______ (ring) a friend.

I ______ (be) a teacher. I ______ (teach) our former president while he ______ (attend) the local school. I ______ (know) him ever since.

While Luke and Anna ______ (kiss) on the bench in the park, someone ______ (break) into their car and ______ (steal) all their money.

Last Christmas, I ______ (get) a new bike.

I ______ (be) in the hospital last summer because I ______ (break) my leg.

Carolyn ______ (love) cherries. Every summer, she ______ (go) to the supermarket and ______ (buy) at least one pound of cherries.

Paul ______ (never / be) to Germany. He ______ (want) to go last spring but he ______ (be) out of money and ______ (can / not) afford to go.

ÜBEN

1.5 Das *future*

Zukünftige Ereignisse und Handlungen können im Englischen mithilfe unterschiedlicher Zeitformen formuliert werden: Man unterscheidet ■ das *going to-future,* ■ das *will-future,* ■ das *future progressive,* ■ das *simple present* und das *present progressive* mit Futurbedeutung und ■ das *future perfect.*	I **am going to buy** a new dress for my best friend's wedding. It **will be** cold in Moscow in January. I **will be writing** an English test tomorrow morning. The train **departs** from platform two. I can't come. I **am tidying up** my room, as I promised. **Will** you **have checked** the battery when I come back?

Das *going to-future*

Das *going to-future* setzt sich aus der Präsensform von *be* + *going to* + Infinitiv zusammen.	I **am going to eat** she **is going to sing**
Es wird verwendet, um ■ Pläne und Absichten zu formulieren oder	We are going to have visitors from California in July.
■ auszudrücken, dass etwas mit großer Sicherheit eintreten wird.	Look at these clouds! It is going to rain soon.

Das *will-future*

Das *will-future* setzt sich zusammen aus dem Wort *will* und dem Infinitiv (ohne *to*) des Vollverbs.	I **will go** she **will drive**
Das *will-future* wird verwendet, um ■ allgemeine Vorhersagen,	All our friends will be there for the wedding.
■ Vermutungen und Hoffnungen oder	I hope he will take me out for dinner tonight.
■ spontane Überlegungen bzw. Entscheidungen zu formulieren.	I'm unhappy. I'll eat a whole box of chocolate candy.
Sätze im *will-future* werden **verneint,** indem zwischen *will* und das Vollverb ein *not* geschoben wird.	I will not go to Sarah's party.
Merke: Die Kurzform von *will not* lautet *won't!*	I won't go to Sarah's party.

Das *future progressive*

Auch vom *will-future* gibt es eine *progressive*-Form: Sie setzt sich zusammen aus *will* + *be* + *-ing*-Form.	I **will be going** he **will be staying**
Das *future progressive* wird verwendet, um ■ in der Zukunft andauernde Ereignisse oder ■ höfliche Nachfragen über zukünftige Pläne zu formulieren.	Professor Smith will be giving another lecture on English literature next term. Will you be staying for dinner?

Das *simple present* mit Futurbedeutung

Das *simple present* kann zukünftige Bedeutung haben, wenn es für feststehende Termine verwendet wird. Deswegen nennt man es auch *timetable future*. Es steht meist nach den Verben *to arrive, to leave, to begin, to start, to end, to open, to close.*	What time does your plane arrive in Los Angeles? The guided tour through the museum starts at the information desk.

Das *present progressive* mit Futurbedeutung

Auch das *present progressive* kann aussagen, dass man etwas in der Zukunft fest geplant hat. In den meisten Fällen verdeutlicht eine Zeitangabe *(tomorrow, on Monday, next week, this summer, every weekend)* diese futurische Bedeutung.	Would you like to see *Pink* in concert next October? – No, I can't. I am travelling to Australia in October.

Das *future perfect*

Das *future perfect* wird mit *will* + *have* + *past participle* gebildet. Es sagt aus, dass Vorgänge, Handlungen oder Zustände zu einem bestimmten Zeitpunkt in der Zukunft abgeschlossen sein werden.	I **will have visited** she **will have caught** When I'm 18 years old, I will have finished school.
Das *future perfect* wird auch verwendet, um Vermutungen und Wahrscheinlichkeiten zu formulieren.	It's no use risking a speeding ticket – the plane will have left by now.

ÜBUNG 14 Trage die unterschiedlichen Futurformen in die Tabelle ein.

infinitive	*will-future*	*future progressive*	*future perfect*
to go			
to catch			
to talk			
to speak			
to write			

ÜBUNG 15 Mrs Miller schreibt für ihre Familie Erinnerungszettel, bevor sie auf Geschäftsreise geht. Vervollständige die Sätze und verwende die richtige Futurform.

Tim, ______ (write) a math exam next Thursday. ______ (not / forget) to study!

Rose, there ______ (be) a concert scheduled for you to play on Wednesday. Please promise that you ______ (practise) every day. And don't forget to ask Sarah whether her Mom or Dad ______ (be able to) take you home. And don't forget your friend's birthday tomorrow. Lisa's mother told me that they ______ (take) you all to the cinema.

Peter, we've invited friends for a barbecue the very evening of my return. You ______ (have to do) the shopping. And you ______ (spend) that afternoon cleaning up the backyard, okay?

I've got to hurry now. My train ______ (leave) at 7.15 a.m. Have a good time. Bye!

ÜBUNG 16 **Am letzten Schultag vor den Ferien unterhalten sich die Schüler und Schülerinnen über ihre Pläne. Verwende die passenden Formen des Futurs, um die Sätze zu vervollständigen.**

Michael: "I _____ (not / study) any vocabulary over the holidays. However, I _____ (stay) with my girlfriend at her aunt's for one week. And as soon as I _____ (finish) school next summer, I _____ (take) my girlfriend on a trip round the world."

Sarah: "I hope it _____ (be) hot all summer. Then I _____ (spend) every afternoon at the swimming-pool. I assume I _____ (get) a good tan *(Sonnenbräune)* then."

Mary: "I _____ (sleep in) every day. And I _____ (do) a lot of shopping around in our shopping centre."

Susie: "My parents and I _____ (spend) two weeks in Greece. I guess we _____ (do) a lot of sight-seeing there."

Sharif: "I _____ (redecorate) my room. Maybe I _____ (make) a new shelf. I hope I _____ (finish) all the work until school starts again."

Monica: "We _____ (host) an exchange student from New Zealand. She _____ (arrive) at London Airport next Saturday. And I _____ (visit) her in New Zealand over Christmas."

Marc: "I _____ (not / do) anything special. I _____ (just relax, see) what happens."

Teacher: "I hope you _____ (enjoy) your holidays. Relax – you _____ (need) a lot of strength as soon as school _____ (start) again on September 1st."

ÜBEN

WISSEN

Verben mit zukünftiger Bedeutung
Einige Verben haben in Verbindung mit dem Infinitiv eines Vollverbs (+ Verb) zukünftige Bedeutung, z. B. *to expect to, to hope to, to want to, to wish to, would like to.*

I expect them to buy the house.
I wish to speak to the manager of this hotel.
She hopes to meet her friend again soon.

to be about to do something:
Diese Wendung drückt aus, dass etwas in sehr naher Zukunft geschieht. Jemand ist fast schon dabei, etwas zu tun.

I am about to cry.
She is about to prepare dinner.

ÜBUNG 17 **Vervollständige die Sätze mithilfe der angegebenen Wendungen.**

to be about to (2x) – to wish to – to expect sb. to do sth.

Don't eat that chocolate now. We ______ have lunch in a minute.

Kate has got good nerves. I ______ pass the driving test easily.

Stop teasing your little sister. Look at her, she ______ cry!

Your exam results are terrible. I ______ speak to your teacher as soon as possible.

ÜBUNG 18 **Mary und Kate sprechen über ihre Pläne für den Abend. Übersetze den folgenden Dialog ins Englische. Schreibe in dein Übungsheft.**

Mary: „Kommst du heute Abend mit auf die Schulparty, Kate? Peter und Marc wollen auch kommen und ich denke, die Party wird richtig gut."
Kate: „Leider werde ich das heute Abend nicht schaffen. Ich habe versprochen, auf meine kleine Schwester aufzupassen. Wenn ich das nicht mache, gibt es Ärger."
Mary: „Wann werden deine Eltern denn wieder zu Hause sein?"
Kate: „Ich weiß es nicht genau. Vielleicht so gegen 22 Uhr?"
Mary: „Die Party dauert bestimmt länger. Komm doch einfach später noch vorbei."
Kate: „Also gut. Ich komme, sobald meine Eltern wieder zu Hause sind."
Mary: „Super! Ich freue mich schon auf heute Abend. Tschüss, Kate!"
Kate: „Bis bald!"

1.6 Die englischen Zeitformen auf einen Blick

■ ***simple present:*** Infinitiv, in der 3. Ps. Sg. mit *-s* am Wortende Signalwörter: *always, sometimes, first, never, often, usually, every ay / week / month* ■ ***present progressive:*** *am / are / is + -ing-*Form Signalwörter: *(right) now, at the moment, just, Look!, Listen!*	They go fishing. Peter likes chocolate. Peter is watching TV at the moment.
■ ***simple past:*** Infinitiv + *-ed* oder unregelmäßige Formen Signalwörter: *last, ago, yesterday, once, used to* ■ ***past progressive:*** *was / were + -ing-*Form Signalwörter: *all day, all week, while*	I hiked Grand Canyon last Sunday. Joey was reading a book all day.
■ ***present perfect simple:*** *has / have been + -ing-*Form Signalwörter: *already, before, (not) yet, never, ever, since, for* ■ ***present perfect progressive:*** *have / has been + -ing-*Form Signalwörter: *how long?, all day / week, for hours*	I have never been to Hawaii. How long have you been waiting for that letter to arrive?
■ ***past perfect:*** *had + past participle* Signalwörter: *after, when, before* ■ ***past perfect progressive:*** *have / has + been + -ing-*Form des Verbs	We had already eaten before our friends arrived. They had been driving for hours when they finally spotted a nice little campground.
■ ***will-future:*** will be + Infinitiv Signalwörter: *tomorrow, next day / week / year* ■ ***going to-future:*** *am / are / is + going to +* Infinitiv ■ ***future progressive:*** *will + be + -ing-*Form ■ ***future perfect:*** *will + have + past participle*	I will fly to California next week. I am going to study medicine when I've got my A levels. Will you be staying overnight? When I am fifty years old, I will have travelled around the world.

ÜBUNG 19 **Setze die richtige Zeitform jeweils in der *progressive*-Form ein.**

Look, the sun ______ (come out).

Paris Hilton ______ (walk) around London with her huge sunglasses for three hours before anybody recognized her.

Since 2003, my sister ______ (live) in New Zealand.

I usually get up at 6.30 but today I ______ (stay) in bed.

While my father ______ (dig) a hole for the gas pipe, he listened to the radio.

ÜBUNG 20 **Verwende das *future perfect*.**

Next year, my husband and I ______ (be married) for ten long and endless years.

Don't worry. The plane ______ (no / leave) before we get to the airport.

Next summer I ______ (work) in the same boring job with the same company for over eight years.

ÜBUNG 21 **Setze die richtige Verbform ein: Verwende das *simple past*, das *past perfect simple*, das *past perfect progressive* oder das *present perfect progressive*.**

Since his wife left him, Peter ______ (cook) his own dinner.

Mickie ______ (practise) karate for two hours now.

Last night, Ashley ______ (not / drink) any beer. Do you think she ______ (be) pregnant?

When you came in with that fancy dress, you ______ (look) like a hippie from the sixties.

I was sick because I ______ to many scoops of ice cream.

It ______ (rain) all day when Sarah ______ (remember) ______ that she ______ (forget) to take the laundry inside.

ÜBUNG 22 **Ein Blind Date – *will-future, going to-future* oder *future progressive?***

Lea: "________ (you / go out) to the party with us next Friday night?"

Hannah: "No, I won't. I ________ (meet) a guy named Johnny. My sister arranged it."

Lea: "What ________ (you / do) all night?"

Hannah: "We probably ________ (have) dinner first. And later we ________ (go) dancing."

Lea: "Do you think you ________ (enjoy) spending your time with a boy you've never met before?"

Hannah: "Well, I hope it ________ (not / be) boring."

ÜBUNG 23 **Setze die richtige Zeitform des Verbs in die Lücken.**

He came into the living room while I ________ (watch) TV.

What are you doing at the moment? – I ________ (prepare) dinner.

Two years ago, while I ________ (travel) through Spain, I ________ (meet) the man who now ________ (be) my husband.

She has ________ (not / read) a book since her baby daughter ________ (be) born last January.

When my grandmother ________ (be) a little girl, she ________ (live) in Hungary.

Yesterday, Annie was late for work because her son ________ (fall) sick.

Our plane to Los Angeles ________ (leave) Frankfurt Airport at 10 o'clock next Monday.

Next January, they ________ (be married) for 15 years.

Kate ________ (visit) her brother three times since he is in hospital.

Carla used ________ (be) a good pupil. However, she ________ (fall) seriously sick last winter and ________ (miss) a lot of lessons, so she now ________ (have) a hard time catching up in all the topics.

ÜBEN

Check-up Die Zeiten

45 Minuten

AUFGABE 1 **Setze die folgenden Verben in die angegebene Zeit.**

we / think *(present perfect simple)* →

I / learn *(past perfect progressive)* →

you / put *(will-future)* →

he / carry *(simple present)* →

she / begin *(future perfect)* →

we / bring *(simple past)* →

we / overtake *(present progressive)* →

you / go *(going to-future)* →

we / laugh *(past progressive)* →

he / speak *(past perfect simple)* →

it / rain *(future progressive)* →

AUFGABE 2 ***Simple present* oder *present progressive?***

It ______ (be) summer. The sun ______ (shine) and it ______ (get) really hot. Sarah ______ (be) on the beach. She ______ (write) a postcard.

Dear Sally,
I ______ (write) these lines on the beach. We usually ______ (spend) our holiday in Great Britain, but it ______ (rain) a lot there. So this year we ______ (spend) our holidays in Spain. At the moment, I ______ (enjoy) the sun, the beach and the ocean. But I ______ (not / like) our hotel: The meals ______ (taste) awful and my bed ______ (smell) of cat droppings ☹. Lots of love, Sarah

TESTEN

AUFGABE 3 ***Simple present* oder *present progressive, simple past* oder *past progressive?***
Setze die angegebenen Verben in die richtige Zeit.

We __________ (go) to Greece two years ago.

This room __________ (smell) terribly. Close the door, please.

Before Mary __________ (go) out for dinner with her boyfriend, she __________ (do) all her homework, __________ (call) her friend, __________ (decide) what to wear and __________ (take) a shower.

Why __________ (you / not / come) to Sarah's party last night? – I __________ (have) a bad headache so I __________ (think) I'd better stay at home.

As a young woman, my Mom used to __________ (play) the guitar.

Be quiet, please. I __________ (listen) to my favourite song.

"What __________ (you / do) at 10 p. m. last night?" my mother __________ (ask) at breakfast.

The Beatles __________ (write) numerous songs.

AUFGABE 4 ***Present perfect simple* oder *progressive?* Wähle außerdem zwischen *since* und *for.***

Kate __________ (be) at school __________ 8 o'clock this morning.

My friends __________ (live) in San Francisco __________ six years now.

I'm awfully cold. I __________ (wait) for the train to arrive __________ half an hour.

Liz __________ (not / study) her vocabulary __________ many weeks. Tomorrow's French test will be very difficult for her.

My parents __________ (know) each other __________ 20 years.

Laura and Hanna __________ (be) friends __________ 2002.

Kim __________ (read) that novel __________ a long time.

Janet and Sarah __________ (talk) on the phone __________ more than one hour now.

AUFGABE 5 **Wähle eine passende Futurform, um die Sätze zu vervollständigen.**

At eight o'clock tonight, this shop ______ (be) closed.

She ______ (not / come) any more. It's too late now.

Sarah's parents argue a lot. I guess they ______ (split up).

My sister is pregnant. I hope she ______ (marry) soon.

We've just bought a big property. By next October, we ______ (live) in our own house.

The fog ______ (clear up) soon.

She ______ (give) a party together with her best friend.

This summer holidays, I ______ (stay) at my aunt's in Australia.

My family ______ (go) to Spain this summer.

______ (you / finish) your homework by 5 o'clock this afternoon?

AUFGABE 6 **Letztes Wochenende warst du auf eine Party eingeladen. Verfasse einen Bericht, in dem du das *past perfect* und das *simple past* verwendest. Schreibe vier Sätze und verwende zweimal *after.***

After I got dressed for the evening, I ______

______

______

______

______

I haven't had such a great evening for a long time.

AUFGABE 7 **Übersetze und schreibe die Sätze in dein Übungsheft.**

Der Mechaniker wird die Geschirrspülmaschine bis Montag nicht repariert haben.
Was werden wir nächstes Jahr um diese Zeit tun?
Sie heiraten im Mai.
Ich habe mir vergangene Woche das Bein gebrochen.
Laura sitzt seit drei Stunden an ihren Hausaufgaben.
Wann fährt der nächste Zug nach London?
In letzter Zeit hat sich in ihrer Firma einiges geändert.

2

Das Passiv

2.1 Die Zeiten im Passiv

Ein Aktivsatz wird zum Passivsatz, indem das direkte Objekt zum *Subjekt* wird. Will man hinzufügen, wer oder was für ein Ereignis bzw. eine Handlung verantwortlich ist, hängt man den *by-agent* an. Das Passiv wird gebildet aus ***to be* + *past participle,*** indem *to be* in die jeweilige Zeitform gesetzt wird.	*Aktiv:* My little sister **asks** a lot of questions. *Passiv: A lot of questions* **are asked.** A lot of questions are asked **by the pupils.**
simple present: *am / are / is + past participle*	I am asked, you are asked, she is asked English is taught three days a week at my school.
present progressive: *am / are / is being + past participle*	I am being asked, you are being asked At the moment, an English test is being written.
simple past: *was / were + past participle*	I was asked, you were asked, he was asked My iPod was stolen yesterday.
past progressive: *was / were being + past participle*	I was being asked, you were being asked I was being asked to host a family from California while the conference took place in our city.
present perfect: *has / have been + past participle* Die *progressive*-Form wird sehr selten verwendet: *has been / have been + -ing*-Form	I have been asked, she has been asked The flowers have just been picked. A movie has been being watched.
past perfect: *had been + past participle* Auch hier gibt es eine sehr selten verwendete *progressive*-Form: *had been + -ing*-Form	I had been asked, he had been asked This exercise had been done before. The flowers had been being watered.
will-future: *will be + past participle*	I will be asked, you will be asked The new car model will be released in May.

ÜBUNG 1 **Bilde die Passivformen dieser Verben in der jeweils angegebenen Zeitform.**

to catch *(present perfect simple)* →

to choose *(simple past)* →

to give *(will-future)* →

to carry *(simple present)* →

to ask *(past perfect simple)* →

to hold *(simple past)* →

to wake up *(present perfect simple)* →

ÜBUNG 2 **Sieh dir die Bilder an: Was passiert gerade? Schreibe jeweils drei Sätze im Passiv und verwende Satzanfänge aus dem Wortspeicher. Aufgepasst: Je nachdem, welchen Satzanfang du wählst, musst du auch die Zeitform ändern!**

last Thursday – at 10 o'clock yesterday – last summer – next spring – for half an hour – never

a) The dog .

→ the dog .

→ .

b) The bank .

→ a bank .

→ .

c) The house .

→ the house .

→ .

ÜBUNG 3 **Verwandle die Sätze vom Aktiv ins Passiv. Achte darauf, jeweils die richtige Zeitform zu verwenden!**

This restaurant accepts traveller cheques.

Not many teachers teach Japanese.

The storm destroyed the boat.

Someone has seen a bear in the forest.

Everybody loves Paul.

ÜBUNG 4 **Unterstreiche im folgenden Text zunächst alle Verben, die hier ins Passiv gesetzt werden können. Setze den Text dann ins Passiv und schreibe ihn neu in dein Übungsheft.**

An awful incident

An old lady has done her shopping and walks home slowly. A young man follows her secretly. As soon as the old lady has unlocked the door of her apartment, the man knocks her down. The criminal enters the apartment, looks through every single room and takes away all valuables *(Wertsachen)*.

Fifteen minutes later, a neighbour discovers the old lady in the corridor. The neighbour calls the police. The paramedics *(Rettungssanitäter)* take the old lady to hospital. A week later, the police catches the thief in a traffic check. He was driving too fast.

ÜBUNG 5 **Hast du in Übung 4 alles richtig gemacht? Vergleiche deinen Text mit der Lösung. Setze dann deine Geschichte in die Vergangenheit. Schreibe in dein Übungsheft und beginne wie unten angegeben.**

Last year, the old lady's shopping **had** been done and she ...

WISSEN +

Das Passiv mit zwei Objekten

Manche Verben ziehen zwei Objekte nach sich, ein indirektes (meist eine Person) und ein *direktes* Objekt (meist eine Sache). Solche Verben sind *to give, to offer, to promise, to show, to sell, to send, to tell.*

My daughter never shows us *her letters.*
Tom tells Tina *a story.*

Mit diesen Verben kann man Passivsätze auf zwei unterschiedliche Arten bilden:

- das *direkte Objekt* eines Aktivsatzes wird zum **Subjekt** des Passivsatzes,
- das indirekte Objekt des Aktivsatzes wird zum **Subjekt** des Passivsatzes.

Her letters are never shown to us.
A story is told to Tina.
We are never shown the letters.
Tina is told a story.

ÜBUNG 6 **Setze die Aktivsätze ins Passiv. Aufgepasst: Bei jedem Satz gibt es zwei Möglichkeiten! Schreibe sie in dein Übungheft.**

My friend told me the news.
Dad bought a new pair of Jeans for Laura.
Grandmother read a book to Meggie.
Peter gave his girlfriend a birthday present.

ÜBUNG 7 **Richard hat sich während der Besprechung der Schülermitverwaltung Notizen gemacht. Am Abend schreibt er einen kurzen Artikel für die Schülerzeitung. Verwende, wo immer möglich, Passivkonstruktionen, und achte auf die richtige Zeit!**

yesterday, 3 p.m. - school party meeting!
headmaster: fixed party date for July 8th two days ago
discussed subjects: food, drinks, games
next meeting: June 15th, 3 p.m. - help wanted!

Yesterday, a meeting was

2.2 Weitere Passivkonstruktionen

Modalverben im Passiv

Auch die modalen Hilfsverben wie *can, could, must, ought to* und *shall* können Passivformen bilden. Es gilt:	
■ Das modale Hilfsverb oder die entsprechende Ersatzform *(to have to, to be able to, to be allowed to)* bleibt unverändert.	You **can change** money here. → Money **can be changed** here.
■ Das Vollverb wird mit *be* und dem *past participle* ins Passiv gesetzt (↑ Kap. 2.1).	Alan **had to carry** his sleeping dog upstairs. → His sleeping dog **had to be carried** upstairs.

Verben mit Präpositionen im Passiv

Viele Verben haben eine Präposition, die fest mit dem Verb verbunden ist, z. B.: *to break into – einbrechen* *to look after – sich kümmern um* *to talk about – sprechen über* *to think of – denken an*	The girls often talk about clothes. → Clothes are often talked about. I have to look after my little cousin Hannah once a week. → Once a week, my little cousin Hannah is looked after by me.
Diese beiden Bestandteile dürfen auch im Passivsatz nicht getrennt werden. Die Satzstellung im Passiv lautet dann: Subjekt + Verb + Präposition + Objekt (+ *by-agent*)	Robbers broke into the house. → The house was broken into.

Infinitivkonstruktionen im Passiv

Auch Sätze mit Infinitiv können im Passiv stehen.	My little brother loves to be tickled *(Präsens).* The parents ought to have been informed *(Perfekt)* about this.
Aufgepasst: Bei einem Satz, in dem *to be* + Passiv steht, handelt es sich um eine Anweisung!	This private property isn't to be walked on.

WISSEN

ÜBUNG 8 **Im Krankenhaus. Setze die angegebenen Hilfsverben und Verben in die richtige Passivform und verwende auch die Ersatzform, wo es möglich ist.**
Beispiel: All patients must be treated / have to be treated (must / to treat) with respect.

The staff ______ (ought to / inform) about all changes in every patient's condition.

The patients ______ / ______ (can / visit) from 10 a.m. until 5 p.m.

All medicine ______ / ______ (must / lock away) in the nurses' office.

All documents ______ (should / handle) confidentially *(vertraulich)*.

Just in case: Forgotten items ______ (to be / take) to the nurses' office.

ÜBUNG 9 **Bilde aus den angegebenen Wörtern Passivsätze mit Verb + Präposition. Achte auf die Verwendung der richtigen Zeit und Wortstellung!**

Jimmy	to break into	last Saturday
The baby	to look at	next month
The new houses	to look after	never
The speech	to listen to	at the moment
This apartment building	to pull down	always
This bank	to make fun of	two days ago

______
______
______
______
______
______

WISSEN +

Das persönliche und das unpersönliche Passiv An das Passiv von Verben des Sagens und Denkens kann ein Infinitiv mit *to* angeschlossen werden. Im Deutschen wird diese Konstruktion am besten mit „man sagt, dass", „von ... heißt es, dass" übersetzt. Man spricht vom **persönlichen Passiv.**	Aleesha is **thought to be** very clever. (Man sagt, Aleesha sei sehr schlau.) Mr Baker **is said to be** a millionaire. (Von Mr Baker heißt es, er sei Millionär.) Many people **are believed to have lost** their homes in the hurricane. (Man glaubt, dass... / Viele Menschen sollen ...)
Für Informationen, die nicht gesichert sind, kann man das **unpersönliche Passiv** verwenden (oft in Zeitungsartikeln). Es wird gebildet mit *it is said / reported that* ... Die Wiedergabe im Deutschen erfolgt wie beim persönlichen Passiv.	**It is said that** he is very rich. ("Es wird gesagt" → Man sagt, dass er sehr reich ist. / Er soll sehr reich sein.) **It is reported that** three pupils from our school intend to participate in ... (Es wird berichtet, dass ... / Drei Schüler sollen ...)

ÜBUNG 10 **Verwende das persönliche oder das unpersönliche Passiv, um die Sätze zu vervollständigen.**

Tom ______________ very sensitive.

The president didn't appear for the talk show. ______________ that he couldn't come because he is quite ill.

Thousands of children ______________ to have lost a close relative in the earthquake in Asia last December.

Last night, a terrible accident happened on the motorway to London. ______________ four people were killed.

ÜBUNG 11 **Übersetze. Schreibe die Sätze in dein Übungsheft.**

Alle Regeln müssen vom Team befolgt werden.
Man sagt, ihr Vater sei ein reicher Mann.
Hanna bekam von ihrem Lehrer viele Fragen gestellt.
Die Nachbarin wird gerade ins Krankenhaus gebracht.
Ich hoffe, dass mir nächstes Jahr ein guter Job angeboten wird.
Als ich letzte Woche von der Schule nach Hause kam, wurde gerade unser Auto abgeschleppt *(to haul away)*.

Check-up Das Passiv

45 Minuten

AUFGABE 1 **Bilde die Passivformen dieser Verben in der jeweils angegebenen Zeitform.**

to tell *(present perfect simple)* →

to spend *(simple past)* →

to bite *(will-future)* →

must find *(simple present)* →

to drive *(past perfect simple)* →

to keep *(simple past)* →

to sing *(present perfect)* →

AUFGABE 2 **Jacob verbringt den Tag mit seiner kleinen Tochter Hanna. Verwandle die Sätze ins Passiv und schreibe sie in dein Übungsheft.**
Beispiel: Jacob takes Hanna along to the supermarket. → Hanna is taken along to ...

Jacob allows her to eat an ice cream.
Jacob takes her to the playground.
Jacob calls Hanna's mum to tell her how nice Hanna is.
Jacob sends her to bed very early.

AUFGABE 3 **Verwandle die Sätze vom Aktiv ins Passiv. Achte auf die richtige Zeit und schreibe die Sätze in dein Heft!**

The neighbour is taking Lea's dog for a walk.
Look! Somebody is washing his car.
Tom didn't feed the fish in the pond.
Somebody had stolen her purse.
Many years ago in first grade, the teacher taught us the alphabet.
My mother often gives away her books.
My friends haven't given me a birthday present so far.

AUFGABE 4 **Setze die richtige Form im *past progressive* in die Lücken.**

The wallpaper ______ (take down) when the phone rang.

A party ______ (hold) when a heavy thunderstorm struck.

An exam ______ (write) when the fire alarm was set off.

TESTEN

AUFGABE 5 **Setze die richtige Zeit in die Lücken: *simple present, present progressive* oder *simple past?***

Some cars ______ (make) with a lot of plastic.

These flowers are really dry. They ______ (must / water) by somebody.

A century ago, most books ______ (read) by more than one reader. Today, a lot of books ______ (never / read) by anybody.

Look! Brad Pitt ______ (film) over there!

The first automobile ______ (invent) by Karl Benz in 1885.

AUFGABE 6 **Setze den folgenden Text ins Passiv. Schreibe anschließend eine Fortsetzung zu dem Text und verwende dabei so viele Passivformen wie möglich.**

An easy life?

As a baby, life is very easy. Parents feed their babies about five times a day and entertain them. And in a lot of families, the grandparents spoil the baby, too. For example, they take it for a walk in its pushchair. Yes, it's true – babies lead an easy life.

But as a teenager, life changes. As we all know, we usually have to look after ourselves! At least, ______

TESTEN

3 Die indirekte Rede

3.1 Der *backshift of tenses*

Die indirekte Rede dient dazu, die Aussage, Ansicht oder Meinung einer Person einem (meist unbeteiligten) Dritten mitzuteilen. Dabei steht am Anfang meist ein einleitendes Verb ***(reporting verb)***, auf das eine Konjunktion *(that – dass, if / whether – ob)* folgt.

Laura **says** **that** she doesn't like math.

Pat **asked** me **if** I wanted to go swimming.

↓ einleitendes Verb ↓ Konjunktion

That kann auch weggelassen werden.

He said he had seen Robbie Williams in the local supermarket.

Steht das *reporting verb* im ***present tense***, wird die Aussage in der indirekten Rede **unverändert** wiedergegeben.

Sue: "Brad Pitt **is** the best-looking actor ever." → Sue says that Brad Pitt **is** the best-looking actor ever.

Aufgepasst: In der indirekten Rede ändern sich die Pronomen stets wie folgt:

- **Personalpronomen:**
  I / you → he / she; we / you → they;
  me / you → him; us / you → them
- **Possessivpronomen:**
  my / your → his / her; our / your → their

Marc: "**We** went to Spain last summer." → Marc says that **they** went to Spain last summer.
Kate: "I play **my** piano every day." → Kate says that she plays **her** piano every day.

Steht das *reporting verb* im ***past tense***, werden die Zeiten in der indirekten Rede **um eine Zeitstufe nach hinten** verschoben. Man nennt dies den *backshift of tenses* (Rückverschiebung der Zeiten):

direkte Rede	→	**indirekte Rede**
simple present	→	*simple past* (1)
present perfect	→	*past perfect* (2)
simple past	→	*past perfect* (3)
going to-future	→	*was / were going to + infinitive* (4)
will-future	→	*would + infinitive* (5)

(1) Sarah: "I like ice cream." → Sarah said that she liked ice cream.
(2) Mary: "I have never been to New York." → Mary said that she had never been to New York.
(3) Peter: "I didn't buy a car." → Peter said that he hadn't bought a car.
(4) Susan: "I am going to go to Mary's party." → Susan said that she was going to go to Mary's party.
(5) Jim: "I'll buy some flowers." → Jim said that he would buy some flowers.

Merke: Bei der Verwendung von *progressive*-Formen gelten diesselben Regeln!

Joe: "She is singing." → Joe said that she was singing.
Brad: "They have been singing." → Brad said that they had been singing.

ÜBUNG 1 **Übersetze die folgenden Verben ins Englische. Überlege dann, was diesen Verben gemeinsam ist, und formuliere einen Merksatz.**

sagen →	say	fragen →	ask
erzählen, sagen →	tell	denken →	think
berichten (über) →	report	erwähnen →	mention

etwas wissen wollen / gespannt sein → wonder

Merksatz: Alle diese Verben können einen Satz in der indirekten Rede einleiten. Es handelt sich um reporting verbs.

ÜBUNG 2 **Unterstreiche die richtige Verbform. Achtung: *backshift* oder nicht?**

Tim: "That's an unbelievable story." → Tim said that that ~~is~~ / was / ~~were~~ an unbelievable story.

Marc: "In my opinion, accounting *(Buchhaltung)* is a boring job for boring people." → Marc states that in his opinion accounting ~~was~~ / is / ~~had~~ been a boring job for boring people.

Kate: "If I ever marry, I will only marry someone rich." → Kate told her friend that if she ~~would ever marry~~ / ever married / ~~had ever married~~, she ~~will only marry~~ / would only marry / ~~had only married~~ someone rich.

Sarah: "My grandfather has become less active during the past months. I hope he won't die soon." → Sarah said that her grandfather ~~became~~ / had become / ~~has become~~ less active during the past months. She added that she hoped / ~~hopes~~ / ~~had hoped~~ he ~~won't~~ / would not / ~~is not~~ die soon.

ÜBUNG 3 **Schreibe die Sätze in der indirekten Rede in dein Übungsheft. Achte auf die richtige Umwandlung der Pronomen!**

Susie told her teacher: "I'm sorry, I didn't understand your explanation, so I didn't do my homework."

Lisa asked: " Have you ever heard of that terrible famine *(Hungersnot)* in Ireland in the early 19th century?"

Tom said: "I had a bad day yesterday. I missed my bus, was late for school and lost my watch on the way home."

WISSEN+

Orts- und Zeitangaben in der indirekten Rede

Auch Orts- und Zeitangaben ändern sich, wenn das *reporting verb* im *past tense* steht:

direkte Rede		**indirekte Rede**
now	→	*then / at the moment*
today	→	*(on) that day*
tonight	→	*that night*
tomorrow	→	*the next / the following day*
yesterday	→	*the day before / the previous day*
last month	→	*the month before / the previous month*
next month / year	→	*the following month / year*
this	→	*that*
here	→	*there*

Morris: "It is Mother's Day **today** in the United States, too." → Morris said that it was Mother's Day **on that day** in the United States, too.

Debbie: "I went to a party **last night.**" → Debbie said that she had gone to a party **the night before.**

Ally: "**This** is my favourite town. I'm going to stay **here** forever." → Ally said that **that** was her favourite town and that she was going to stay **there** forever.

ÜBUNG 4 **Wandle die Sätze in die indirekte Rede um. Wann tritt *backshift* ein, wann nicht? Achte auch auf die Veränderung der Orts- und Zeitangaben! Schreibe die Sätze in dein Übungsheft.**

The Millers say: "We go out for dinner once a week."
"Do you like reading?" the teacher asked his pupils.
Susan says: "I haven't studied my English vocabulary in a while. But we'll be writing a test next week, so I'd better study them tonight."
Lucy told her friend: "I met a nice boy at the disco last night."
The teacher said: "We will go on a one-week school trip to London next March."
Laura said: "I have never been to San Francisco before. But my younger sister travelled to San Francisco last May."
Laura states: "Melanie's party starts at 7.30 p.m. tonight."
Rob says: "I'll buy a new mobile phone next month."
Anne told Mary: "I met our maths teacher at that Italian pizza place yesterday."
Cynthia told her boyfriend: "It's my Chinese grandma's birthday today. She is going to celebrate here in England."
Aunt Helen asked: "I haven't seen your mother today. Where did she go?"

ÜBUNG 5 **Die Schüler haben Informationen zur bevorstehenden Klassenreise bekommen. Zu Hause berichtet Simon, worüber gesprochen wurde.**

Simon: " This morning at school, our teacher told us that

ÜBUNG 6 **Finde die sechs Fehler in diesen Sätzen. Unterstreiche sie und schreibe die ganzen Sätze richtig in dein Übungsheft. Tipp: Ein Satz ist richtig!**

ACHTUNG FEHLER

Journalists believed that more newspapers are sold at weekends when you have enough time to sit and read for hours.

Today it is widely accepted that Canadian Inuit and Indians ~~were~~ are proud of having been their country's first inhabitants.

It is said that Christopher Columbus discovered America in ~~1692~~ 1492. (Achtung Falle!)

My mother said to me that most TV programmes ~~are~~ were not really worth watching. (Zwei Fehler!)

The girl said that she was just eating chocolate.

It is said that in Shakespearean times women ~~had~~ were not allowed to perform on stage.

ÜBEN

3.2 Modale Hilfsverben in der indirekten Rede

Grundsätzlich gilt: Auch die modalen Hilfsverben ändern sich in der indirekten Rede, wenn das *reporting verb* im *past tense* steht. Die Veränderung folgt dabei festen Regeln:

will	→	*would* (1)
can	→	*could* (2)
may	→	*might* (3)
shall	→	*should* (4)

(1) Peter: "I will help you in the kitchen." → Peter said (that) he would help me in the kitchen.
(2) Mary: "I can read that traffic sign here. Can you, too?" → Mary wondered whether I could read that traffic sign there, too.
(3) Father: "I may need a new pair of trousers for Sarah's wedding." → Father said that he might need a new pair of trousers for Sarah's wedding.
James: "Shall I lend you a hand?" → James asked if he should lend his friend a hand.

Aufgepasst: Wird ***shall*** in der 1. Person verwendet, bleibt es in der indirekten Rede
- entweder unverändert oder
- wird mit *would* wiedergegeben.

Jim: "I shall be delighted to meet your parents." → Jim said that he shall be / would be delighted to meet my parents.

Das modale Hilfsverb ***must***
- kann unverändert bleiben, wenn ein Vorschlag, eine Annahme oder eine Schlussfolgerung ausgedrückt werden,
- wird durch *had to* ersetzt, wenn es eine Verpflichtung ausdrückt.

Cynthia: "You must be our new teacher." → Cynthia said that he must be their new teacher.
Teacher: "You must welcome your new classmate." → The teacher said we had to welcome our new classmate.

Für das modale Hilfsverb ***mustn't*** gilt in der indirekten Rede:
- Es bleibt entweder unverändert oder
- wird durch *shouldn't / wasn't / weren't to* ersetzt.

Father: "You mustn't watch TV at midnight!" → Father said that I mustn't / shouldn't / wasn't to watch TV at midnight.

Das modale Hilfsverb ***needn't***
- bleibt unverändert oder
- wird durch *didn't have to* ersetzt.

Mum: "You needn't do the dishes tonight." → Mum said that I needn't / didn't have to do the dishes that night.

Achtung: Would, could, might, should und *ought to* bleiben unverändert!

Laura: "I ought to see the dentist." → Laura said that she ought to see the dentist.
Kate: "I would go to the cinema tonight if I had some money left." → Kate said that she would go to the cinema that night if she had some money left.

ÜBUNG 7 **Jeweils eines der drei Modalverben kann unverändert bleiben, wenn das *reporting verb* im *past tense* steht. Unterstreiche es.**

a) shall / will / may
b) can / must / will
c) ought to / may / can

ÜBUNG 8 **Wandle die Sätze in die indirekte Rede um. Verwende immer ein einleitendes Verb im *past tense*. Schreibe in dein Übungsheft.**

Gary: "Shall we go out for dinner next Saturday?"
Mother: "You mustn't eat so much chocolate."
Bank manager: "You must pay back the money this month."
Peter to Kate: "You must be tired after running the marathon."
Teacher: "You needn't worry about your school report."
Tom: "I'm sure I will enjoy my holidays."
Coach: "I may need some help with the junior team."
The sign said: "You mustn't eat ice cream while riding the tram."

WISSEN+

Fragen und Aufforderung

Für Fragen gelten die gleichen Regeln wie für Aussagesätze. Es steht kein Fragezeichen. Fragen ohne Fragewort werden in der indirekten Rede mit *if* oder *whether* formuliert.	Rita: "Lisa, when did you buy this t-shirt?" → Rita wanted to know when Lisa had bought that t-shirt. Tom: "Did you see the latest film with Angelina Jolie, Rob?" → Tom asked if / whether Rob had seen the latest film ...
Aufforderungen und Befehle werden mit einem **Infinitiv mit *to*** wiedergegeben. Das gilt auch für Angebote, Einladungen oder Bitten.	Teacher: "Be quiet." → The teacher told us to be quiet. Anne: "I'll study hard." → Anne promised to study hard.

ÜBUNG 9 **Wandle die Fragen in die indirekte Rede um.**

Mary: "Jodie, where did you meet your boyfriend for the first time?"

Michael: "Tom, have you ever been to Los Angeles?"

Jasmin: "Maggie, did you see Mrs Miller's new glasses? They look very expensive."

Daneesh: "Peter, will you come to Mike's party next weekend?"

ÜBUNG 10 **Setze die folgenden Sätze in die indirekte Rede. Verwende dabei jeweils ein Verb aus dem Wortspeicher.**

to tell – to warm – to advise – to threaten – to promise

Anne: "I'll buy a new book for you."

Amy: "Don't eat too many chillis. They are very hot *(scharf)*."

Father: "I'll take away your computer if you don't pass your exam."

My older sister: "Lay the table, please."

ÜBUNG 11 **Übersetze die folgenden Sätze und schreibe sie in dein Übungsheft.**

Jane sagte, dass Peter schlecht in Biologie sei.
Meine Eltern sagen, dass sie erst spät nach Hause kommen werden.
Vicky sagte, dass ihr schlecht sei.
Theresa erzählte Marco, dass sie in Mathe einen Test geschrieben haben.
Meine Mutter wollte wissen, wo die Party stattfinden würde.
Sie fragte mich, ob ich mit ihr einkaufen ginge.

Check-up Die indirekte Rede

45 Minuten

AUFGABE 1 ***Backshift of tenses*** **– vervollständige die Tabelle.**

direkte Rede		indirekte Rede
past progressive	→	present progressive
could	→	can
present tense	→	*past tense*
going to-future	→	was / were going to
will - future	→	*would + infinitive*
mustn't	→	might not
don't have to	→	*didn't have to*

AUFGABE 2 **Unterstreiche jeweils die richtige Verbform. Aufgepasst: In einem Satz versteckt sich außerdem eine falsche Zeitangabe! Streiche sie an und verbessere sie.**

Nikos: "I haven't seen my Greek relatives for ages."

→ Nikos said that he wouldn't see / saw / hadn't seen his Greek relatives for ages.

Sue: "I'm going to play chess all day."

→ Sue says that she will play / is going to play / is playing chess all day."

Morris: "I'll be enjoying my work even at age 85."

→ Morris stated that he would be enjoying / was enjoying / enjoys his work even at age 85.

Peter: "Where were you last night?"

→ Peter wanted to know where we have been / had been / were last night.

AUFGABE 3 **Partyregeln – im Jugendzentrum gelten Regeln, die alle Besucher einhalten müssen. Schreibe die Sätze in die indirekte Rede um und verwende als einleitendes Verb *to promise* oder *to be told.***
Beispiel: We promise to / we are told to handle the stereo with care.

PARTY RULES

Be polite to all guests within the premises.

Don't insult other people.

Don't fight with other party guests.

Help your fellows when necessary.

Don't drink and drive!

AUFGABE 4 **Wandle die Sätze in die indirekte Rede um. Schreibe in dein Übungsheft.**

Charles said: "I think I know this book."
Megan says: "I haven't had an ice cream for a while."
Michelle told Anne: "My friend from Germany will be visiting in July."
Tom said: "My father went on a hike which he had often done before."
Laura asked her little sister: "Have you seen our rabbit anywhere lately?"
Rachel said: "I didn't go to my piano lesson this afternoon because I felt sick."
Mother to Lily: "You are not allowed to go to the party tonight."
Amy asked Leo: "Will we see each other next year?"
James said to us: "I'm just preparing lunch."

AUFGABE 5 **Übersetze und schreibe die Sätze in dein Übungsheft.**

Melanie riet mir, zum Arzt zu gehen.
Meine Tante wollte wissen, ob wir nächsten Sonntag zum Mittagessen kommen würden.
Sie beschwerte sich darüber, dass sie so wenig Bücher zum Lesen hätte.
Cara sagte, dass sie 2004 in ihr Haus eingezogen sei.
Ken wollte wissen, welches Team gewonnen hatte.
Die Mutter befahl den Kindern, ihr Zimmer aufzuräumen.
Der Lehrer sagte zu seinen Schülern, dass sie am nächsten Tag einen Ausflug machen würden.
Sie sagte, sie habe drei Jahre in China gelebt.

Der Satz

4.1 Bedingungssätze

Ein Bedingungssatz *(conditional sentence)* besteht immer aus zwei Teilen:
- dem ***if*-Satz,** in dem die Bedingung für ein Geschehen genannt wird, und
- dem **Hauptsatz,** der die Folge eines solchen Geschehens beschreibt.

If you invite Lisa to your party *(if-Satz / Bedingung)*, Mary won't come *(Hauptsatz / Folge)*.

Der Bedingungssatz Typ I

Ist die Bedingung im *if*-Satz **erfüllbar** oder **wahrscheinlich,** handelt es sich um einen Bedingungssatz Typ I. Es steht im:

if-Satz	Hauptsatz
simple present	*will-future* / modales Hilfsverb + Infinitiv

If we travel by plane, our trip will be expensive.

If it rains, I won't water the garden.
If it is a hot day, one can sunburn easily.

Der Bedingungssatz Typ II

Ist die Bedingung im *if*-Satz nach Ansicht des Sprechers **nicht erfüllbar** bzw. **nicht wahrscheinlich,** handelt es sich um einen Bedingungssatz Typ II. Es steht im:

if-Satz	Hauptsatz
simple past	*would / could / might* + Infinitiv

If I won the lottery, I would fly to Hawaii.
If I were my sister, I would move to New Zealand.
If I moved to New Zealand, I would buy a big property there.

Der Bedingungssatz Typ III

Ist die Bedingung im *if*-Satz nach Ansicht des Sprechers **nicht mehr erfüllbar,** weil sie sich auf ein vergangenes Ereignis oder Geschehen bezieht, handelt es sich um einen Bedingungssatz Typ III. Es steht im:

if-Satz	Hauptsatz
past perfect	*would / could / might + have + past participle*

If it hadn't rained, the open air concert would have lasted for hours.
If I had known that, we would have called to inform you.
She would never have begun to learn Latin if she had known how difficult it was.

ÜBUNG 1 **Übersetze die folgenden Funktionswörter ins Englische. Überlege, was diesen Wörtern gemeinsam ist, und formuliere einen Merksatz.**

wenn, falls → if

es sei denn → unless

vorausgesetzt, dass → provided that

angenommen, dass → supposing that

Merksatz: Konjundktionen, die Bedingussätze einleiten können.

ÜBUNG 2 **Kreuze hinter jedem Satz an, um welchen Typ von Bedingungssatz es sich handelt.**

	Typ I	Typ II	Typ III
a) If I moved to London, I would speak English all day.		X	
b) If you turn the handle, the door opens.	X		
c) If you buy that huge wardrobe, you will need a bigger room.	X		
d) If you loved chocolate, you would enjoy that cake.		X	
e) If I had saved some money, I would have flown to Australia.			X

ÜBUNG 3 **Betrachte Satz b) aus Übung 2 genauer und versuche, ob du erklären kannst, warum es sich um einen Bedingungssatz Typ I handelt, obwohl kein *will* steht.**

II + III treffen nicht zu, da es eine feststehende Aussage ist.

ÜBUNG 4 **Beantworte die Fragen mithilfe eines Bedingungssatzes.**
Beispiel: Shall I leave my umbrella at home? – No. (rain) →
No. If you leave your umbrella at home, it will rain.

Is Laura going to study Spanish with her Dad? – No. (quarrel)
Is Mary going to work at an airport? – No. (be able to speak more languages)
Why didn't you spent the night with your friends? – (not / go to school the next day)

ÜBUNG 5 **Verwandle die Aufforderungen in die drei Typen von Bedingungssätzen und schreibe sie in dein Übungsheft.**
Beispiel: Buy this dress! Feel like a princess! → *Typ I:* If you buy this dress, you will feel like a princess. – *Typ II:* If you bought ... – *Typ III:* If you had bought ...

a) Try our super sweet chocolate! Never forget the taste!
b) Don't drink and drive! Be safe!
c) Hike New Zealand! Enjoy the wilderness!
d) Colour your life with Wonder-Colour! Feel better!

ÜBUNG 6 **Bilde Bedingungssätze aus den Satzteilen.**

travel / I / Los Angeles – visit Hollywood *(Typ I)*

If I travel to L.A., I will visit Hollywood.

the Louvre / see / you – be / to know / in Paris *(Typ II)*

If you saw in the Louvre, you would be know in Paris.

the Berlin wall in the 80s / see / you – feel uneasy / you *(Typ III)*

If you had seen the Berlin wall in the 80's, you would have felt uneasy.

protest / you / against lower wages – you / get fired *(Typ II)*

If you protested against lower wages, you would get fired.

she / come / Athens / one day – she / walk up the hill / to visit the Acropolis *(Typ I)*

If she comes to Athens one day, she will walk up the hill to visit the Acropolis.

read / that travel book / I – know / I / the museum / be closed on Wednesdays *(Typ III)*

If I had read that travel book, I would have known that the museum was closed on Wednesdays.

ÜBUNG 7 **Übersetze und schreibe die Sätze in dein Heft.**

Wenn ich die Prüfung bestanden hätte, hätte sich mein Vater nicht aufgeregt.
Können wir morgen einen Schneemann bauen, falls es schneit?
Meine Freundin hätte sich ihr Bein nicht gebrochen, wenn sie in den Ferien zu Hause geblieben wäre.
Wenn die Firma verkauft würde, würden viele Mitarbeiter arbeitslos werden.

4.2 Relativsätze

Relativsätze sind Nebensätze, die durch ein Relativpronomen *(who, which, that, whose)* eingeleitet werden.	
■ ***Who / whom*** bezieht sich auf eine Person,	This is the boy **who / that** has a broken leg. My granddad was a man **who(m)** many will remember as a friend.
■ ***which*** bezieht sich auf Dinge. Sowohl *who* als auch *which* können durch ***that*** ersetzt werden.	We have a house **which / that** is just big enough for our huge family.
Das Relativpronomen ***whose*** kann bei Personen und bei Dingen stehen. Es gibt eine Zugehörigkeit bzw. einen Besitz an.	That's the girl **whose** aunt lives in New Zealand.

Notwendige Relativsätze

Relativsätze, die für das Verständnis eines Satzes unerlässlich sind, heißen notwendige Relativsätze *(defining relative clauses)*. Sie stehen immer **ohne Komma!**	She was the girl who saved her sister's life. It was my boyfriend who gave me this awful present.
Gehört zum Prädikat des Relativsatzes eine **Präposition,** dann steht diese meist **nach dem Vollverb.**	Is this the job that you applied for? That's the book that we have been talking about.
Ist das Relativpronomen das Objekt eines notwendigen Relativsatzes, kann es weggelassen werden. Solche Relativsätze bezeichnet man als ***contact clauses.***	The girl (who) Peter took out for dinner was very beautiful. Is there anything (that) I can do for you?

Nicht notwendige Relativsätze

Liefert der Relativsatz Informationen, die weggelassen werden können, ohne dass sich der Sinn des Hauptsatzes ändert, handelt es sich um einen nicht notwendigen Relativsatz *(non-defining relative clause).* Nicht notwendige Relativsätze werden immer durch ein **Komma** vom Hauptsatz getrennt!	Sometimes my grandmother, **who** is now 72 years old, gets on my nerves. We watched the movie "A Beautiful Mind", **which** I hadn't seen before.

ÜBUNG 8 **Ergänze die fehlenden Relativpronomen im Text und setze Kommas, wo sie notwendig sind.**

My aunt Pam ______ had given me a ticket for the *Pink* concert ______ went to see the show, too. The tram ______ we took to get to the arena ______ was loaded with young people ______ were talking about pop stars and rock concerts. At the entrance my aunt met a friend ______ she hadn't seen in a while. She ______ usually doesn't talk a lot ______ couldn't stop chatting. She told her friend ______ had travelled 400 km to come to the concert ______ the story of her life and vice versa. And guess what? My aunt's friend knew someone from the concert crew and had got back-stage passes! So at the end, my aunt and I got backstage passes, too! My aunt ______ was even more excited than I was ______ made my day: I talked to Pink herself! It's unbelievable, isn't it?

ÜBUNG 9 **Verbinde die beiden Sätze mithilfe eines passenden Relativpronomens. Setze Kommas, wo sie nötig sind.**

My Dad cooked this wonderful meal. He likes to eat.

______

Madame Monique is married to a physician. She is our French teacher.

______

The book is boring. I found it on the underground.

______

My boyfriend gave me tickets for the pop concert. I like him very much.

______

The boy is talking to Jane. He is her brother.

______

Ronald Reagan was a movie star. He was president of the USA, too.

______

ÜBEN

ÜBUNG 10 **Verbinde die Satzteile zu ganzen Sätzen, indem du das richtige Relativpronomen benutzt. Schreibe die Sätze in dein Übungsheft.**
Beispiel: a teacher – works at a school → A teacher is a person who / that works at a school.

a hotel	does magic
a dog	can transport a group of people
a fairy	attracts visitors
Ireland	is built for travellers
an old castle	can be a good friend
a bus	has a shamrock *(Kleeblatt)* as a symbol

ÜBUNG 11 **Verbessere die Sätze, indem du das falsche Relativpronomen durchstreichst und durch das richtige ersetzt. Setze Kommas, wo diese notwendig sind.**

ACHTUNG FEHLER

That's the tram who I usually take.

Where is the girl whom wants to become a movie star?

That's the boy that mother is Italian.

Is this the magazine who you were talking about?

Brazil is not the only country who has a good football team.

My Dad and I saw our favourite football team win that made us very happy.

ÜBUNG 12 **Übersetze.**

Das Haus, das Marys Eltern gehört, sieht aus wie ein Palast.
Ist das der Junge, der Einrad *(unicycle)* fahren kann?
Ist das das Mädchen, deren Eltern Ärzte sind?
Menschen, die rauchen, können ihrer Gesundheit schaden.
Geld, das für Bildung ausgegeben wird, ist eine gute Investition.

ÜBEN

4.3 Sätze mit Gerundium, Infinitiv und Partizip

Das Gerundium im Satz

Das Gerundium *(gerund)* wird durch Anhängen von *-ing* an den Infinitiv des Vollverbs gebildet. Es kommt in vier Formen vor: ■ im Präsens Aktiv und Passiv, ■ im Perfekt Aktiv und Passiv.	to see → see**ing,** to love → lov**ing,** to put → putt**ing** seeing – being seen having seen – having been seen
Im Satz wird das Gerundium ähnlich wie ein Substantiv verwendet. Es kann also **Subjekt** oder **Objekt** sein.	**Swimming** *(„wer oder was?" → Subjekt)* is good for your health. I like **swimming** *(„wen oder was?" → Objekt)* in the ocean.
Zahlreiche **Verben** mit oder ohne **Präposition** haben das Gerundium nach sich: *to admit – to agree with – to apologize for – to avoid – to begin – to complain about / of – to concentrate on – to consider – to cope with – to decide against – to defend – to delay – to deny – to depend on – to detest – to die of – to discuss – to dislike – to dream about / of – to enjoy – to excuse – to finish – to give up – to go on – to imagine – to keep – to like – to mind – to miss – to need – to practise – to resist – to stop – to suggest – to understand*	I apologize for not helping you. He dreamt of buying a house in the countryside. They gave up looking for her lost purse. Would you mind helping me with the dishes? Can you imagine travelling in space?
Bestimmte **Substantive,** die eine **Präposition** bei sich haben, fordern ebenfalls den Gebrauch des Gerundiums: *alternative to – chance of – danger of – demand for – dislike for / of – doubt about – experience in – interest in – invitation to – method of – possibility of – problem of – reason for – trouble in*	They have an interest in arriving at the wedding on time. She has a lot of experience in driving a truck. There's only a small chance of winning the match now.
Das Gerundium steht bei bestimmten **Ausdrücken** und **Redewendungen** wie: *after – before – by – for – instead of – on – without – can't stand / help, it's no use – it's no good – to be busy – to be worth – to spend / to waste time – how about ...?*	Before going out, she finished her work. It's not worth buying that book. How about spending the weekend in New York?

WISSEN

Der Infinitiv im Satz

Mithilfe einer Infinitivkonstruktion (mit oder ohne *to*) kann im Englischen ein Sachverhalt verkürzt ausgedrückt werden. Das gilt insbesondere für Verben des Denkens, Wünschens, Aufforderns, Veranlassens und Verursachens: *to advise – to ask – to believe – to consider – to encourage – to expect – to force – to imagine – to order – to permit – to persuade – to teach – to tell – to warn*	My mother wanted me to help her do the dishes. Father allowed me to go to the party. We heard them argue over money.
Der Infinitiv mit *to* steht auch nach ■ Gefühlsadjektiven, ■ Superlativen, ■ Zahlwörtern sowie nach ■ *right, wrong, easy, hard, difficult, certain* und *welcome*.	They were delighted to hear about her good school report. Mara was the best dancer to perform on stage that night. It's not easy to learn the rules of baseball.
Merke: Es gibt einige Verben, die entweder mit einem Gerundium oder mit einem Infinitiv stehen können, ohne dass sich die Bedeutung ändert: *to begin – to bother – to continue – to hate – to intend – to love – to start.*	She loves eating / loves to eat chocolate. I intend to go / intend going shopping. He started to get / started getting on my nerves.

Das Partizip im Satz

Das Partizip Präsens *(present participle)* wird wie das Gerundium durch Anhängen von *-ing* gebildet. Es kann ■ einen Relativsatz ersetzen, wenn es nach einem Substantiv steht, ■ wie ein Adjektiv verwendet werden.	to talk → **talking,** to sing → **singing** The girl performing (= who performs) on stage is my sister. the working poor
Das Partizip Perfekt *(past participle)* kann ■ vor einem Substantiv einen Relativsatz ersetzen oder ■ nach einem Substantiv einen Relativsatz ersetzen, wenn das *past participle* selbst durch eine (adverbiale) Bestimmung der Zeit oder des Ortes erweitert wird.	the recently arranged meeting (= the meeting which / that was arranged recently) Photos taken on Mars (= that were taken on Mars) were transmitted to the earth.

ÜBUNG 13 **Richtig oder falsch? Kreuze an, ob die Sätze richtig oder falsch sind. Verbessere die Fehler und schreibe die Sätze richtig in dein Übungsheft.**

	right	wrong
How about to travel to Hawaii next summer?		
There must be a reason for cooking potatoes.		
Ian spent a lot of time to try to find a birthday present for his girlfriend.		
He hates living in the countryside.		
He hates to live in the city.		
This morning, she left the house without to eat breakfast.		

ÜBUNG 14 **Gerundium oder Infinitiv? Ergänze die richtige Verbform.**

My parents don't allow me ______ (watch) TV late at night.

I wondered what ______ (buy) for her birthday.

How about ______ (eat out) tonight?

She has a lot of experience ______ (teach).

She opened the window in order ______ (let) some fresh air in.

My brother loves ______ (hike) in the Alps.

The pupils concentrate on ______ (write) their exam.

WISSEN +

***used to* + Infinitiv und *used to* + Gerundium**

Wird ***used to*** mit einem **Infinitiv** verwendet, so wird ein Zustand / eine Gewohnheit in der Vergangenheit beschrieben, die nicht mehr existiert. Diese Sprechabsicht lässt sich auch mit *would* ausdrücken.

Steht hinter ***to be used to*** ein **Gerundium**, bedeutet die Formulierung „gewohnt sein, etwas zu tun".

Peter **used to get up** early when he worked at the bakery. But Peter quit the job.

When I lived in Berlin, I **would go out** a lot = I **used to go out** a lot.

I used to live in a small town. I had to move to New York and I just cannot get **used to living** in that big city.

ÜBUNG 15 **Bedeutungsunterschiede gibt es nicht nur bei *used to,* sondern auch bei anderen Verben. Welche Übersetzung ist richtig? Schlage in deiner Grammatik nach, wenn du dir unsicher bist.**

a) Mein Freund hat aufgehört zu rauchen.

- ☐ My boyfriend stopped smoking.
- ☐ My boyfriend stopped to smoke.

b) Früher ist er immer zeitig aufgestanden.

- ☐ He used to get up early.
- ☐ He is used to getting up early.

c) Wir versuchten, die Schlüssel zu finden.

- ☐ We tried to find the keys.
- ☐ We tried finding the keys.

d) Letzten Winter habe ich Snowboarden ausprobiert.

- ☐ I tried to snowboard last winter.
- ☐ I tried snowboarding last winter.

e) Ich muss daran denken, Tee einzukaufen.

- ☐ I must remember to buy some tea.
- ☐ I must remember buying some tea.

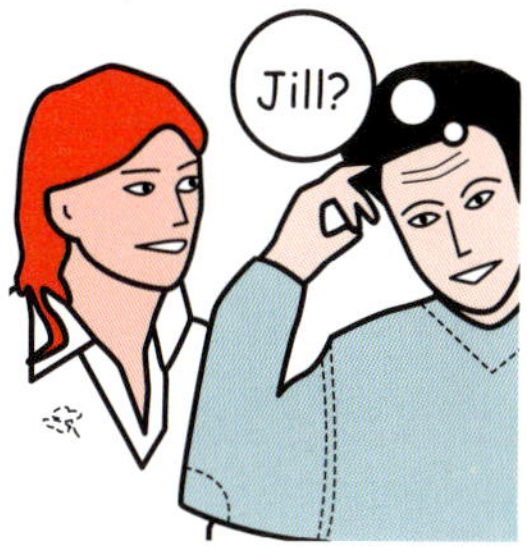

f) Du hast vergessen, dass du Jill getroffen hast, oder?

- ☐ You forgot meeting Jill, didn't you?
- ☐ You forgot to meet Jill, didn't you?

ÜBUNG 16 **Ändere die farbig markierten Verben zu einer Partizipialkonstruktion. Aufgepasst: Bei der wörtlichen Rede musst du außerdem die indirekte Rede (↑ Kap. 3) verwenden! Schreibe den vollständigen Text in dein Übungsheft.**
Beispiel: When Jane *bought* a novel at her favourite bookstore, she noticed that one of the customers was watching her closely. → Buying a novel at ..., Jane noticed ...

But Jane had made up her mind and was determined to buy that book. As she went to the cashier's desk, she threw a glance at that customer. He was getting ready to walk up to the cashier's desk, too. Jane had paid for the book and was walking out onto the street. The customer followed Jane and called after her. "Excuse me," the young man said to her, "but I would like to ask a question: Why did you buy that book?" "Well, a good friend of mine recommended it to me," Jane answered. "Oh thanks," the young man said. "I am the author of this book."

Check-up Der Satz

45 Minuten

AUFGABE 1 **Welcher Ausdruck passt nicht in die Reihe? Streiche ihn durch und begründe deine Entscheidung.**

How about ...? – to waste time – to allow – to be worth

Begründung:

typical of – danger of – method of – experience in

Begründung:

to imagine – to detest – to consider – to expect

Begründung:

AUFGABE 2 **Setze die passende Präposition ein.**

They have been dreaming ______ buying a house since 1998.

My parents have an interest ______ gardening.

Most immigrants have difficulties ______ finding a good job.

My brother must have a reason ______ being so helpful with the dishes.

AUFGABE 3 **Bilde Bedingungssätze und schreibe sie in dein Übungsheft.**

to get married / one day / you – to play the violin / I *(Typ I)*
Sarah / to read / the book – not to go / to the movie / she *(Typ III)*
to meet / Brad Pitt / you – to ask / you / for an autograph *(Typ II, question!)*
to break her leg / my mother / not – she / to travel / to Italy *(Typ III)*
you / to read / that travel guide – you / to know / a little more about California *(Typ II)*

AUFGABE 4 **Füge die richtigen Relativpronomen ein und setze Kommas, wo sie notwendig sind. Achtung: Ein Satz kommt ganz ohne Relativpronomen aus!**

Our school ______ is located across a wonderful park ______ is old but beautiful.

It was my sister ______ gave me tickets for the rock concert.

The people ______ I work with ______ are very nice.

Last week, I took my little niece to the cinema ______ is just around the corner from where I live.

TESTEN

AUFGABE 5 **Infinitiv oder Gerundium?**

It's not worth ________ (to buy) that book. It's boring.

My mother forced me ________ (to study) some English vocabulary.

Dad permitted Hannah ________ (to go) to the party on Saturday.

Would you mind ________ (to help) me with the dishes?

I can hardly resist ________ (to eat) another ice cream.

Instead of ________ (to watch) TV you had better go swimming!

Children usually love ________ (to play) games.

Cara was the best pupil ________ (to play) the violin.

AUFGABE 6 **Verkürze die Sätze mithilfe einer Partizipialkonstruktion.**

When we arrived at our friends' house, we were welcomed by their two little children.

____

As he noticed that the old lady felt sick, Jim called an ambulance.

____

My grandfather, who hasn't worked in the garden for a while, felt tired after mowing the lawn.

____

Mary, who had eaten too much chocolate, felt awful.

____

AUFGABE 7 **Übersetze. Schreibe die Sätze in dein Übungsheft.**

Wenn ich mehr Geld hätte, würde ich öfter im Ausland einkaufen gehen.
Es war falsch, die Kinder alleine zum Einkaufen zu schicken.
Wenn du in der Schweiz leben würdest, müsstest du jeden Nachmittag zur Schule gehen.
Meine Schwester hat aufgehört zu rauchen.
Es hat keinen Sinn, sich über einen schlechten Lehrer zu beschweren.
Jim wollte wissen, welches Team das Spiel gewonnen habe.
Sarah ist es gewohnt, jeden Tag eine Stunde Geige zu üben.
Früher bin ich gern zur Schule gegangen. Aber seit wir eine neue Direktorin haben, macht die Schule keinen Spaß mehr.

5.1 *Useful phrases* in Diskussionen

Eine **Diskussion** ist ein Meinungsaustausch über bestimmte Fragen mit dem Ziel, den Gesprächspartner von der eigenen Meinung zu überzeugen.

Eine Diskussion beginnen

Die **Ausgangssituation** oder das jeweilige Thema / Problem *(subject)* sollte **knapp** und **verständlich** dargelegt werden:

- Welcher sachliche Hintergrund *(facts)* liegt vor? (Problembeschreibung) (1)
- Ist das Problem aktuell? Warum? (2)
- Persönliche Betroffenheit bzw. persönlichen Bezug zum Thema herstellen (3).

(1) Today's topic is ... – To start off with, here is my proposition. – As words of introduction, I say ... – Let me communicate the following facts.
(2) Of relevance in the present situation is the fact that ... – Recently, ...
(3) Of great interest to me is the fact that ... – To my mind ...

Eine Diskussion führen

Im **Mittelpunkt** einer Diskussion steht immer das **Abwägen von Meinungen und Gründen:**

- Das Thema wird in seinen unterschiedlichen Aspekten beleuchtet (1).
- Pro- und Kontra-Argumente *(statements)* werden geordnet (↑ Seite 60) gegenübergestellt (2).
- Argumente werden begründet, z. B. durch Expertenmeinungen oder mithilfe von Tatsachenmaterial *(proof)* (3).

(1) Many people think ... because / although ... – We mustn't forget that ... – We have to keep I mind that ... – There is no denying the fact that ...
(2) The advantages / disadvantages of sth. – on the one hand ..., on the other hand ...
(3) There is enough evidence to show ... – This is proof enough to conclude that ... – Statistics show that ...

Eine Diskussion beenden

Am **Ende** werden alle genannten Argumente **zusammengefasst** und möglichst eine persönliche **Meinung** *(attitude)* oder ein Kompromissvorschlag formuliert *(conclusion)*.

It is for these reasons that I think that ...
I have come to the conclusion that ...
I'd like to finish by saying / suggesting ...
To my mind / in my opinion ...

ÜBUNG 1 **Ein Kreuzworträtsel.**

1 a conversation about something
2 spoken or written words that give information or an opinion
3 any kind of (written) information that shows that something is true
4 something that is known to be true or something that can be proved

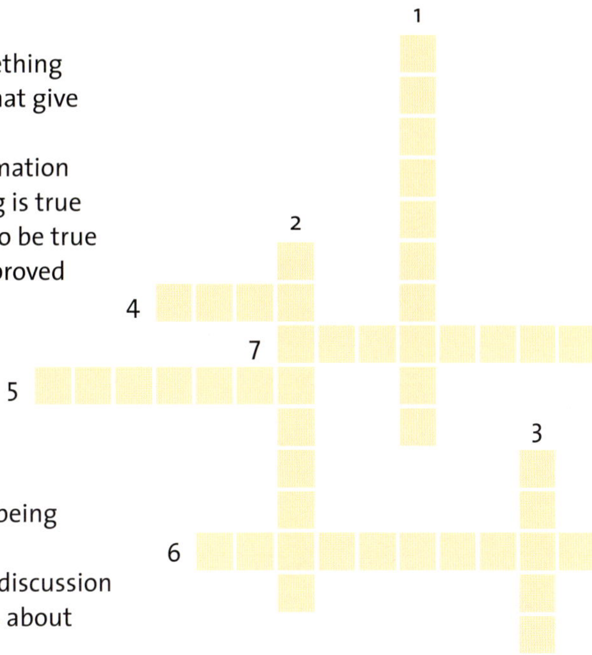

5 a thing or a person that is being discussed
6 the result or outcome of a discussion
7 the way one thinks or feels about somebody / something

ÜBUNG 2 **Mit den folgenden Sätzen kann man jemandem zustimmen, widersprechen oder seine Meinung erfragen. Trage die angegebenen Sätze richtig in die Tabelle ein.**

That's quite right. – How do you feel / think about this? – I don't think that's right. – I may be wrong but … – That's my view exactly. – I can't agree with you more. – What is your view on the matter? – I agree (entirely). – Do you agree with that? – ~~I don't agree at all~~. – That's not the way I see it. – Would you like to add anything?

Zustimmung äußern	Ablehnung äußern	Meinung erfragen
	I don't agree at all.	

WISSEN

Argumente ordnen

In einer guten Argumentation werden die Argumente **nach ihrer Wichtigkeit steigend** aneinandergereiht. Das schlagkräftigste Argument nennst du zum Schluss – was nämlich am Ende einer Diskussion gesagt wird, bleibt am besten im Gedächtnis.

Better don't smoke because smoking
(1) makes your skin look older,
(2) minimizes your lung capacity,
(3) can cause lung cancer,
(4) can make you die earlier.

ÜBUNG 3 **Die Reihenfolge ist hier durcheinandergeraten. Sortiere den Text so, dass er einen Sinn ergibt und schreibe ihn in dein Übungsheft.**

Driving at the age of 16?

[1] As I'm going to be sixteen next month, this question is of great interest to me. – **[2]** However, a proposition has been made recently that 16-year-old teenagers should be able to take driving lessons so that they can take their driving test at the age of seventeen. – **[3]** Many people think that 16-year-old-teenagers are not mature enough to drive. – **[4]** Today, German teenagers are allowed to take their driving test at the age of eighteen. – **[5]** They are convinced that more accidents would happen if younger people were allowed to drive. – **[6]** On the one hand I must admit that they are partly right – not every 16-year-old really is mature enough. – **[7]** And on top of all that, public transport can be very lousy at the weekend and at night – a car could reduce young people's temptation to hitchhike, which is a big danger in itself. – **[8]** However, that can be true for older drivers, too: Some people might just never be mature enough to drive. – **[9]** I'd like to finish by saying that I hope to be able to take my driving test soon. – **[10]** Furthermore, 16-year-olds are already allowed to take a driving test for motorcycles – which are much more dangerous than cars. – **[11]** Motorcycles only have two wheels, thus *(somit)* the driver needs a good sense of balance. – **[12]** In bad weather conditions, driving a motorcycle is dangerous because roads become slippery. – **[13]** Therefore, driving a car would be the better – and less dangerous – alternative. – **[14]** For example, a lot of harm is done by people who drink and drive – alcohol makes driving dangerous, no matter how old someone is.

5.2 Wortfelder und Wortfamilien

Ein **Wortfeld** *(word field)* bezeichnet eine Gruppe von Wörtern, die inhaltlich sinnverwandt sind. Sie werden aus einem Oberbegriff *(group term)* und den dazu passenden Unterbegriffen gebildet.	banana, cherry, apple, pear → fruit jeans, shirt, shorts, glove → clothes
Eine Gruppe von Wörtern, die sich aus der gleichen Wurzel entwickelt haben, bezeichnet man als **Wortfamilie.** Mithilfe verschiedener Vorsilben *(prefixes)* oder Nachsilben *(suffixes)* entstehen aus einem Wortstamm neue Wörter.	*Wortfamilie* "back": back (Rücken), backpack (Rucksack), back end (hinteres Ende), background (Hintergrund) usw. *Wortfamilie* "family": family (Familie), familiar (vertraut), familiarity (Vertrautheit), family tree (Stammbaum), to familiarize (sich vertraut machen) usw.

Vorsilben *(prefixes)*

■ *dis-, in, im-, il-, ir-, non-* und *un-* bezeichnen das Gegenteil,	**dis**advantage, **in**capable, **im**mobile, **ir**relevant, **non**-toxic, **un**believable
■ *anti-* und *pro-* drücken Ablehnung oder Zustimmung aus,	**anti**-war, **pro**-democracy
■ *inter-, sub-* und *trans-* stellen einen örtlichen Bezug her,	**inter**continental, **sub**way, **trans**port
■ *ex-, post-, pre-* und *re-* sind Vorsilben mit zeitlichem Bezug,	**ex**-husband, **post**-war, **pre**cede, **re**store
■ *over-, sub-* und *super-* drücken eine höhere oder niedrigere Stellung aus.	**over**looking, **sub**human, **super**store

Nachsilben *(suffixes)*

■ Wird *-(a)tion, -sion, -ment, -ance/-ence, -ness* oder *-(i)ty* an ein Verb gehängt, entsteht ein abstraktes Substantiv,	to dictate – dict**ation,** clever – clever**ness,** to transmit – transmis**sion,** to assess – assess**ment,** to perform – perform**ance,** real – real**ity**
■ *-ful/-less, -ous, -y, -able* und *-ic* sind Nachsilben, die ein Adjektiv bilden.	harm – harm**ful,** irony – ironi**c,** nerves – nerv**ous,** health – health**y,** to rely – reli**able**
■ Nachsilben, mit denen ein Verb gebildet werden kann, sind *-ize* und *-en.*	harmony – to harmon**ize,** length – to length**en**
Wörter, die die gleiche Bedeutung haben, heißen **Synonyme** *(synonyms).* Mit **Antonymen** *(antonyms)* sind die gegenteiligen Begriffe eines Wortes gemeint.	to sleep – to be asleep, to doze – to take a nap beautiful – ugly, small – tall, fire – water, sky – earth

ÜBUNG 4 **Finde den passenden Oberbegriff für die Wortgruppe.**

castle – lighthouse – pyramid – monastery →

carrot – tomato – cucumber – lettuce →

bungalow – apartment building – semi-detached house – cottage

→

basketball – rugby – gymnastics – high jump →

drill – screwdriver – hammer – handsaw →

ball – doll – stuffed animal – marbles →

ÜBUNG 5 **Nur eine Antwort ist richtig. Kreuze sie an.**

a) Welche Wortbildung ist die richtige, um das Gegenteil von *fortunate* auszudrücken?

- infortunate
- disfortunate
- unfortunate
- imfortunate

b) Wie lautet das zu *violent* gehörige Substantiv?

- violation
- violence
- violin
- violet

c) Wie heißt das zu *terror* gehörige Adjektiv?

- terrorist
- terrible
- terrorize
- terrify

d) Wie heißt das Substantiv zu *true?*

- truly
- truism
- truth
- trust

e) Welches Substantiv zu *clear* gibt es nicht?

- clearance
- clearness
- clarity
- clearence

f) Welche Wortbildung für das Gegenteil von *active* ist zulässig?

- disactive
- irractive
- inactive
- unactive

g) Welches der folgenden Wörter bildet keine Ableitung auf -able?

- fashion
- health
- respect
- count

ÜBUNG 6 **Finde das passende Synonym oder Antonym.**

a) Ein Synonym für *reliable* ist

- trustworthy
- remarkable
- reluctantly
- confidential

b) Das Antonym von *strange* ist

- peculiar
- funny
- common
- surprising

c) Ein Synonym für *polite* ist

- policy
- respectful
- rude
- politics

d) Wie lautet das Synonym für das Verb *practise?*

- practical
- economical
- exercise
- preach

WISSEN +

Wortzusammensetzungen

Werden Wörter unterschiedlicher Wortarten kombiniert, spricht man von Wortzusammensetzungen (Komposita). Solche Komposita können aus den unterschiedlichsten Wortarten bestehen.

fat-free *(Substantiv + Adjektiv)*
garden-party *(Substantiv + Substantiv)*
greenhouse *(Adjektiv + Substantiv)*
good-looking *(Adjektiv + Partizip)*

ÜBUNG 7 **Die folgenden Wörter sind durcheinandergeraten. Setze sie richtig zusammen und schreibe sie in deinem Übungsheft auf.**

every, swimming, drug, apple, fire

horse, breath, home, friend, green

proof, beauty, pine, pool, witness

check, girl

taking, made, body

rocking, house

double, candle, eye, queen, store

ÜBUNG 8 **Bearbeite die folgenden Fragen in deinem Übungsheft und vervollständige dann den Text mit den angegebenen Begriffen im Kasten.**

a) Wie lautet das Verb zu *visitors?*
b) Welche Wortart ist *remote?*
c) Finde ein Synonym zu *aircraft!*
d) Bilde zwei Komposita mit *any.*
e) Wie heißt das Substantiv zu *accessible?*
f) Nenne ein Antonym zu *quickly.*

visitors – accessible – remote – quickly – any – advice – graves – illness – comprehensive – institutions – aircraft

The Royal Flying Doctor Service of Australia

Australia is a very large country with quite some people living in ______ areas. Thus, modern infrastructure, especially health care ______, hospitals etc., haven't been easily ______ for all of Australia's inhabitants und can still cause some problems. About a century ago, serious ______ or accidents often meant death. The Australian inland holds many lonely ______ of people who might have lived, had they been able to receive medical aid ______ enough. Therefore, in 1928, the RFDS was founded. The service soon provided medical aid in emergencies and also a ______ primary health care to those living in the outback. Today, the RFDS is a very modern organization. ______ make about 80 % of the country accessible within two hours, and medical ______ is provided via radio telephone at ______ time, day or night. And in cases of serious illness or accidents, emergency flights are made. Until today, the RFDS is there to help the people – the people living in the outback as well as the many ______ and tourists travelling a wonderful continent!

5.3 *False friends*

Die englische und die deutsche Sprache haben gemeinsame Wurzeln, daher stimmen viele Wörter auch in ihrer Bedeutung überein. Solche Wörter helfen dir, die Bedeutung eines Wortes in der Fremdsprache zu erschließen.	alphabet (engl.) → das Alphabet (dt.) person (engl.) → die Person (dt.) shoe (engl.) → der Schuh (dt.)
Einige Wörter im Englischen aber sind deutschen Wörtern sehr ähnlich, haben jedoch eine ganz andere Bedeutung. Diese sogenannten **falschen Freunde *(false friends)*** musst du dir besonders gut merken!	sensible (engl.) → vernünftig (dt.) sensibel (dt.) → sensitive (engl.)
Merke: Wenn die gedachte Bedeutung des deutschen Wortes in dem Zusammenhang, in dem es dir begegnet, keinen Sinn ergibt, handelt es sich mit hoher Wahrscheinlichkeit um einen *false friend!*	The fire brigade usually uses a very thick **hose** to extinguish a fire. (Die Feuerwehr verwendet normalerweise eine ziemlich dicke ~~Hose~~ → einen ziemlich dicken **Schlauch,** um ein Feuer zu löschen.)
Es gibt unzählige *false friends.* Zu den häufigsten gehören:	
actual ≠ aktuell: actual → tatsächlich; aktuell → current	eine **aktuelle** Frage → a **current** issue, *nicht:* an ~~actual~~ issue
critic ≠ Kritik: critic → Kritiker; Kritik → criticism	He couldn't cope with the criticism, *nicht* with the ~~critic~~.
eventually ≠ eventuell: eventually → schließlich; eventuell → perhaps	Meine Großmutter bekam ein **Rezept** für ein besonderes Schmerzmittel. → My grandmother got a **prescription** for a special painkiller.
meaning ≠ Meinung: meaning → Bedeutung; Meinung → opinion	Kannst du mir das **Rezept** für den leckeren Schokoladenkuchen aufschreiben? → Can you write down the **recipe** for that delicious chocolate cake?
ordinary ≠ ordinär: ordinary → gewöhnlich; ordinär → vulgar	
rent ≠ Rente: rent → Miete; Rente → pension	

ÜBUNG 9 **Achtung: *false friends!* Schlage die englischen Wörter in deinem Wörterbuch nach und suche dann die richtige Übersetzung für das falsche, aber ähnliche deutsche Wort.**

ordinary	→	personal	→
ordinär	→	Personal	→
rent	→	receipt	→
Rente	→	Rezept	→
to wonder	→	chips	→
sich wundern	→	Chips	→

ÜBUNG 10 **In jedem Satz steckt ein Fehler. Unterstreiche ihn und ersetze den falschen Begriff durch den richtigen. Erstelle dann eine Liste mit den falsch verwendeten Begriffen und übersetze diese.**

ACHTUNG FEHLER

Tim can't take any kind of critic. He always overreacts. →

What's the actual score? – It's 2:3 for our team. →

The murder could escape easily. →

At the moment, I'm reading Harry Potter books. It's a very interesting lecture.

→

The department store's personal is taking a trip to the castle tomorrow.

→

Sarah has worked very hard this term, and indeed, her notes have improved a lot.

→

Jeans are hoses that can be worn on many occasions. →

Kate wondered when Kevin told her about his problems. He had never done that before. →

Die falsch verwendeten Begriffe und ihre richtige Übersetzung:

ÜBUNG 11 **Setze das richtige englische Wort in die Lücken.**

How much is the *(Miete)* ______ for this flat?
Your *(Kritik)* ______ of his work is not justified. He has done it quite well.
What's your *(Meinung)* ______ of the new film? – I didn't like it at all.
I really don't understand why the *(Kritiker)* ______ has written such a positive article.
Can you tell me the *(Bedeutung)* ______ of that sign over there? – It tells you that you're not allowed to use your *(Handy)* ______.
I really don't know why he doesn't talk to me anymore. *(Eventuell)* ______ he is still angry because I didn't go out with him last weekend.
Most teenagers know exactly which ______ *(Marke)* of sneakers they want to wear.

ÜBUNG 12 **Setze richtig in die Lücken ein.**

a) except / accept: Everybody was happy to ______ the invitation – everybody ______ Jamie who had rather gone to see the football match.
b) principal / principle: Some pupils don't like the new ______ because she always judges according to very strict ______.
c) own / owe: After living in a small apartment for five years, the Millers now ______ a house – but they ______ quite some money to the bank, too.
d) self-conscious / self-confident: Peter is a very good guitar player. He could be ______, but he has always been ______ about being red-haired.

ÜBUNG 13 **Übersetze und schreibe die Sätze in dein Übungsheft.**

Mein Großvater bekommt nur eine kleine Rente.
Es ist nicht sehr vernünftig, bis nachts um drei Uhr fernzusehen.
Hast du schon jemals für *Unicef* gespendet?
Die Vermieterin verlangte zusätzlich zur Miete eine Kaution *(deposit)*.
Die aktuelle Ausgabe dieser Zeitschrift berichtet über einen großen Skandal.

5.4 Wörterbucharbeit

Je schwieriger die englischen Texte werden, die im Unterricht drankommen, desto wichtiger ist es, mit einem Wörterbuch umgehen zu können.

Das zweisprachige Wörterbuch

Zweisprachige Wörterbücher sind zweiteilig. In der einen Hälfte findest du die Übersetzung vom Englischen ins Deutsche, in der anderen Hälfte ist es umgekehrt. Ein zweisprachiges Wörterbuch informiert neben der Übersetzung außerdem über:

- die Aussprache in phonetischer Lautschrift (in eckigen Klammern), — tomb raider: [tuːm 'reɪdə(r)]
- die Silbentrennung, — dec·or·ate; re·al·ity
- die jeweilige Wortart, — vb = verb; n = noun; adj = adjective, adv = adverb
- grammatikalische Besonderheiten, — information [U] = uncountable word
- Wortzusammensetzungen. — milk: milkman, milk shake, milk tooth

Wird das jeweilige **Stichwort** *(headword)* eines **Eintrags** *(entry)* im erklärenden Text erneut genannt, wird es durch ein Auslassungszeichen, die **Tilde** (~), ersetzt.

place: Ort; I can't be in two ~s at once: Ich kann nicht an zwei Orten gleichzeitig sein.

Das einsprachige Wörterbuch

In einem einsprachigen Wörterbuch wird das englische Wort auf Englisch erklärt. Du kannst damit zwar nicht vom Deutschen ins Englische übersetzen, dafür aber lernst du die Fremdsprache besser.

knowledge (of / about sth.): the information, understanding and skills that one gains through education and experience

Ein einsprachiges Wörterbuch liefert dir die gleichen Informationen wie ein zweisprachiges, enthält aber außerdem **Beispielsätze** und gibt **Redewendungen** an.

frying pan: shallow pan with a long handle used for frying; to jump out of the ~ into the fire: to go from a bad situation to one that is worse

ÜBUNG 14 **Leitwörter: In einem Wörterbuch steht auf der linken Seite oben das erste Wort der Seite links, auf der rechten Seite oben das letzte Wort der Seite rechts. Ein Wort passt jeweils nicht zwischen die folgenden Leitwörter. Streiche es durch.**

disgrace – dispiriting:	disobedient – disgust – dishwasher – disk – discuss
familiar – farm:	farewell – fan club – family – false – far
horse – house:	hot – horror – host – hour – hostility
keyboard – king:	kill – kick – key – kind – kilo
life – light:	lift – light – lie – lightning
ocean – off:	odd – occur – odour – ocelot – of

ÜBUNG 15 **Schlage das Wort *exercise* in deinem Wörterbuch nach und beantworte die folgenden Fragen.**

a) Wie lautet die korrekte Aussprache von *exercise?* Schreibe in Lautschrift.

b) Welcher Wortart bzw. welchen Wortarten kann *exercise* zugerechnet werden?

- [ ] adjective
- [ ] verb
- [ ] noun
- [ ] adverb

c) Gibt es einen Plural von *exercise?* Gib ein passendes Beispiel an!

d) Übersetze den Begriff *physical exercise!*

ÜBUNG 16 **Vervollständige die Tabelle. Erinnere dich an die Wortbildungsregeln von Kap. 5.2 und schlage die Wortfamilien gegebenenfalls in deinem Wörterbuch nach.**

	Substantiv	Verb	Adjektiv
engl.	acceptance	to accept	acceptable
dt.			
engl.	ache		
dt.			
engl.		to deepen	
dt.			
engl.			studious
dt.			

ÜBUNG 17 **Welche Lautschrift gehört zu welchem Wort? Verbinde, was zusammengehört.**

rɪˈzʌlt | bəʊl | words | apologize

result | favour | ˈɔːfl | ˈfeɪvə(r)

ˈtʃeɪndʒ | əˈpɒlədʒaɪz | bowl

awful | wɜːdz | change

WISSEN+

Was sonst noch im Wörterbuch steht

Im **Anhang** eines Wörterbuchs findest du

- die wichtigsten grammatischen Erklärungen,
- eine Liste der unregelmäßigen Verben,
- Vorschläge für Briefformulierungen,
- Angaben zu englischen und amerikanischen Maß- und Gewichtseinheiten, zu Zahlen, Datums- und Uhrzeitangaben.

Aufgepasst: In manchen zweisprachigen Wörterbüchern befindet sich dieser Anhang in der Mitte des Wörterbuchs, wo der deutsch-englische Teil auf den englisch-deutschen Teil trifft.

ÜBUNG 18 **Benutze dein Wörterbuch, um die folgenden Fragen zu beantworten.**

a) An welcher Stelle steht in einem englischen Brief die Absenderangabe?

☐ oben links ☐ einzeilig am unteren Seitenrand ☐ oben rechts

b) Was bedeutet die Wendung *to whom it may concern?*

c) Wie viel *feet* sind ein *yard?* Und wie viel sind ein *yard* im metrischen Längensystem?

1 feet = 1 yard =

d) Was bedeutet der Begriff *ounce?* Mache genaue Angaben und nenne die metrische Entsprechung.

ÜBEN

Check-up Wortschatz

45 Minuten

AUFGABE 1 **Wie lautet das zum jeweiligen Adjektiv gehörige Substantiv? Nimm notfalls dein Wörterbuch zu Hilfe.**

clear →
real →
brilliant →
funny →
long →

AUFGABE 2 **Wie lautet das zum jeweiligen Substantiv zugehörige Verb?**

comparison →
quotation →
harmony →
height →
director →
assistant →

AUFGABE 3 **Welches ist das richtige Wort? Kreuze an.**

If a doctor is convinced that some medicine might help, he writes a

- receipt
- prescription
- recipe

The workers of a company are called

- pension
- personal
- staff

If you are asking for a new job, the person who finally decides is called the

- chief
- boss
- chef

Scientists usually work in a

- labour
- laboratory
- bureau

TESTEN

AUFGABE 4 **Erkläre die folgenden Begriffe auf Englisch. Dein Wörterbuch hilft dir.**

to mention →

to agree →

to propose →

to persuade →

suggestion →

attitude →

AUFGABE 5 **In jedem Satz ist ein falsches Wort versteckt. Verbessere die Sätze mithilfe deines Wörterbuchs und schreibe sie richtig in dein Heft.**

ACHTUNG FEHLER

My sister is very good in swimming.
She is very timid to find a new job.
My brother's face was red from anger when he came home from school.
I want proof for your love. Give me a kiss now!
I'm sorry for your bad test results.
We are late for the game. But I'm sure that somebody can tell us the actual score.

AUFGABE 6 **Die folgenden Sätze helfen dir dabei, eine Diskussion auf Englisch zu führen. Ordne die Begriffe aus dem Wortspeicher in die Tabelle ein.**

I view that as ... – This does not appeal to me. – Yes, indeed. – Sorry, but that's nonsense. – I my opinion, it's a good thing to ... – We need a more balanced view. – All right. – That's my view exactly. – I wouldn't have thought ... – That's not the way I see it. – Definitely! – I can't agree with you.

contradicting	agreeing	reacting to information

6.1 Mündliche und schriftliche Sprachebenen

Je nachdem, mit wem du dich unterhältst: Die **Wortwahl** ist entscheidend, wenn du in verschiedenen Situationen angemessen kommunizieren möchtest.
Wer eine Fremdsprache beherrschen will, muss deshalb nicht einfach nur Wörter wissen, sondern sie auch **situationsbezogen** sowie **stilistisch** und **idiomatisch richtig** aus dem Gesamtwortschatz auswählen und anwenden können.
Im schriftlichen Gebrauch wird eher das formelle Englisch *(formal English)* verwendet, im mündlichen das informelle *(informal English)*.

Peter to his friend: "Hey, shut up. I'm watching TV."
Peter to his father: "Dad, would you please stop talking? I'm watching TV."

formal English	*informal English*
to assist	to help
to extinguish	to put out
I'm of the opinion ...	I'm sure ...
I couldn't agree more.	Right you are.
I'm uncertain.	You're kidding. / I don't believe you.

Formal and informal English

Das *formal English* zeichnet sich durch die folgenden Besonderheiten aus:

- Das unpersönliche Passiv ermöglicht es dem Sprecher, den Sachverhalt bzw. das Thema gleich zu Beginn eines Satzes zu benennen.

formal: The work done by immigrants ...
informal: The work that has been done ...

- Auf den Gebrauch des Personalpronomens *you* wird verzichtet; stattdessen steht das unpersönliche *one*.

formal: One has to wash hands before meals.
informal: You have to wash hands ...

- Nominalisierung, Verwendung von Gerundien,

formal: After having done my homework, I can go out and see my friends.
informal: After I have done my homework, I can go and see my friends.

- die Verwendung des Konjunktivs, der ansonsten im Englischen nur sehr selten vorkommt.

formal: I think it is best that my daughter studied more vocabulary.
informal: I think my daughter had better study more vocabulary.

ÜBUNG 1 **Finde zu dem formellen Begriff eine informelle Entsprechung. Schlage gegebenenfalls in deinem Wörterbuch nach.**

formal words / phrases	informal equivalent
to encounter	
gratified	
Would you please stop talking?	
assistance	
to menace	
We would like people to be quiet now.	
I couldn't agree more.	
What I am trying to express is ...	
I am uncertain.	
I don't entirely disagree, but ...	
to elucidate	
to extinguish (a fire)	

ÜBUNG 2 **Finde zu dem jeweiligen informellen Wort oder Ausdruck eine Entsprechung oder Erklärung in *formal English* und übersetze dann den Ausdruck.**

to get cold feet →

( )

to dawn on somebody →

( )

drivel →

( )

to be for the birds →

( )

He was struck dumb. →

( )

ÜBUNG 3 **Überlege, welche Situation welche Stilebene erfordert. Schlage die Begriffe aus dem Wortspeicher in deinem Wörterbuch nach und ordne sie dem passenden Sprechanlass zu. Tipp: Einen Begriff musst du doppelt verwenden!**

elevated – vulgar – sophisticated – stilted – colloquial – slangy – familiar

Gesetzestext *(law text):*

offizielle Einladung *(letter of invitation):*

ein Leserbrief an eine Jugendzeitschrift *(a letter to the editor of a youth magazine):*

Jugendliche im Gespräch untereinander *(youngsters among their peers):*

Flüche *(swear words):*

politische Rede *(political speech):*

Lexikoneintrag *(entry in an encyclopaedia):*

Brief an ein Familienmitglied *(letter to a family member):*

ÜBUNG 4 **Peter hat seinen ehemaligen Kollegen John getroffen. Am nächsten Tag erzählt er einem anderen Kollegen von der Begegnung. Formuliere seine Aussage um: Wie würde Peter sich a) einem guten Freund, b) seinem Chef gegenüber ausdrücken?**

Peter: "Do you remember John? I met him yesterday and he told me he is planning to go to Australia. I wonder if he's ever been there."

a) Zu seinem Freund sagt Peter:

b) Seinem Chef berichtet Peter:

ÜBEN

WISSEN +

Stilmittel und Klangfiguren

Stilmittel *(stylistic / rhetorical devices)* und Klangfiguren *(sound devices)* werden eingesetzt, um einen bestimmten **Effekt** zu erzielen, z. B. etwas zu veranschaulichen, hervorzuheben oder eine Spannung zu erzeugen. Zu ihnen gehören u. a.:

- *alliteration:* Wiederholung der Anfangskonsonanten,
- *euphemism:* beschönigender Ausdruck,
- *metaphor:* indirekter oder bildhafter Vergleich,
- *parallelism:* Wiederholung eines Satzbaumusters,
- *repetition:* Wiederholung,
- *symbol:* Sinnbild,
- *rhetorical question:* rhetorische Frage zur Hervorhebung einer Tatsache.

alliteration: **P**eter and **P**aul
euphemism: to pass away (*instead of* to die)
metaphor: a heart of stone
parallelism: Laura likes **hiking, singing and swimming.**
repetition: The safety of our children **depends on** watchful adults. And in everyday traffic, it also **depends on** car seats and similar devices.
symbol: The rose is a symbol for love.
rhetorical question: Shall I compare thee to a summer's day? (*Shakespeare,* Sonnet 18)

ÜBUNG 5 **Ergänze die passenden Begriffe.**

metaphor – repetition – alliteration – symbol – rhetorical question – parallelism

The cross is a ______ for Christianity.

The repeated use of a word or word group in order to emphasize an important aspect is called ______.

A question which is not followed by an answer as the answer is obvious is called a ______.

a figure of speech implying an indirect comparison → ______

The repeated use of a syntactical structure in a sentence or in neighbouring sentences is called ______.

If the initial sounds are repeated at the beginning of or in the middle of neighbouring words for rhythmic effect, we talk of ______.

6.2 Situationsgemäß formulieren

Mithilfe von **Satzmustern** lassen sich manche Sachverhalte treffender formulieren.	
Vergleiche kannst du so formulieren: ■ *less / more ... than,* ■ *the + comparative ... the + comparative,* ■ *it's + superlative ... present perfect + ever.*	There is less money in my purse today than there was yesterday. The more I eat, the heavier I grow. It's the best film I've ever seen.
Für **Zugeständnisse** eignen sich: ■ *although + main clause,* ■ *in spite of / despite + noun / gerund + main clause,* ■ *it doesn't matter how / what ... + main clause.*	Although the car is fast, it doesn't consume much petrol. Despite eating all the time, she doesn't gain any weight. It doesn't matter how hard I work, I will never pass the exam.
Ratschläge lassen sich mithilfe von ■ *had better + infinitive without to* oder ■ *it's worth + gerund* ausdrücken.	We had better leave at once or we'll be late. It's worth learning languages.
Absichten mit einem erwünschten Ergebnis formulierst du mit: ■ *main clause + so as (not) to ...,* ■ *to do (something) to prevent (someone) from + gerund* oder ■ *for + noun / pronoun + to + infinitive.*	We studied hard so as to pass our exams. We must do everything to prevent our neighbours from moving. I'll leave some money for you to buy yourself something to drink.
Ergebnisse lassen sich mithilfe von *such ... that* formulieren.	He was such a good swimmer that he won the first prize.
Eine **Ursache** stellt man durch ein *present participle* dem Hauptsatz voran.	Being rich and beautiful, she managed to become a movie star.
Einen **Wunsch** oder eine **Vorliebe** sprichst du aus, indem du an ■ *to wish* einen abhängigen Nebensatz hängst oder ■ *if only* mit einem Hauptsatz verwendest.	I wish you were here. If only I had married rich.
Redewendungen lernst du am besten auswendig, denn ihre Bedeutung ist meist unabhängig von der Einzelbedeutung eines jeden Wortes. Ein Vorrat an **idiomatischen Wendungen** erleichtert dir die Alltagskonversation.	to make a mountain out of a molehill (aus einer Mücke einen Elefanten machen) Let me just get a note pad to write it down. (Ich hole schnell etwas zu schreiben.)

ÜBUNG 6 **Formuliere vollständige Sätze aus den vorgegebenen Satzteilen, indem du auf die Satzmuster von Seite 77 zurückgreifst.**

often / than / less money / earn / expect / you

long – more / stay / London / like / the city / I

not much money / although / I / want / buy / bike

had better / work / hard / he

to be worth / visit / London

bought / I / a piece of cake / her / try

if only / larger room / I / have

suggest / I / a party / have

not matter / it / love Pamela / he / not to be going / she / him / marry

I / most boring book / be / ever read

such + that / bad handwriting / not read / can / the address / I / it / be

can fly / I / wish / to the moon

ÜBUNG 7 **Übersetze die folgenden Redewendungen. Schlage gegebenenfalls in deinem Wörterbuch nach.**

that is to say →

to lose heart →

to drop someone a line →

to cut a long story short →

as the saying goes →

The early bird catches the worm. →

It's raining cats and dogs. →

ÜBUNG 8 **Finde eine angemessene englische Redewendung.**

Ich bin ganz Ohr. →

eine Stecknadel fallen hören →

Ich habe ein Hühnchen mit dir zu rupfen. →

das Herz auf dem rechten Fleck haben →

Halte mich auf dem Laufenden. →

ÜBUNG 9 **Mit den folgenden *phrases* kann man Aussagen abschwächen *(downtoners)* oder eine knappe Antwort formulieren *(rejoinders)*. Sortiere sie entsprechend ihrer Aussage in die folgende Tabelle.**

Very well! – What I meant was … – Am I right in thinking …? – I'm not saying that. What I am saying is … – All right! – Please. – Come on. – What about you? – I'm wondering if / whether … – I beg your pardon? – Am I to understand …? – Certainly. – Of course!

interrupting an argument	agreeing with an argument	clarifying

6.3 Sprachliche Mittel zur Hervorhebung

Um etwas besonders zu betonen, stehen dir im Englischen verschiedene sprachliche Mittel zur Verfügung.	
do / does + infinitive: Wird in einem Satz *do* oder *does* dem Verb vorangestellt, wird dadurch die Aussage besonders hervorgehoben. Im *past tense* steht *did*.	I **do like** chocolate. I **did sleep** well last night – although I didn't have a cushion.
***no* vor Substantiv:** Wird *no* vor ein Substantiv gestellt, erfährt dieses dadurch eine besondere Betonung.	**No** human being always tells the truth. **No** amount of washing his hands could remove Macbeth's guilt of committing murder.
really: Im Sinne von „tatsächlich" hat das Wort *really* emphatische Wirkung, ähnlich wie *totally – total* oder *pretty – ziemlich.*	The two of you don't look alike at all. Are you **really** sisters? He's **totally** out of his mind. Linda is **pretty** clever, isn't she?
***yet* in der Satzmitte:** Steht das Wörtchen *yet* nicht am Satzende, sondern in der Satzmitte, kommt der Aussage besondere Bedeutung zu.	I have not **yet** read a better book.
zero* anstelle von *no: Wird in einer Aussage *no* durch *zero* ersetzt, wird die Bedeutung dieser ohnehin schon betonten Aussage zusätzlich verschärft.	The coach insists: **zero** alcohol before World Cup matches.
it: Wird *it* (meist in Verbindung mit einer Form von *be*) an den Satzanfang gestellt, betont man damit die folgende Aussage.	**It** was the deep green colour of her eyes that made her face so very attractive.
what: In Verbindung mit *most* hebt auch *what* eine Aussage hervor.	**What** I liked **most** about her was her serenity *(Heiterkeit).*
Voranstellungen: Wird eine Aussage, z. B. durch eine Partizipialkonstruktion, an den Satzanfang gerückt, kommt ihr eine besondere Bedeutung zu.	**Being poor,** he couldn't afford to go to university. **Because of its smoothness,** silk is highly estimated in making clothes.

ÜBUNG 10 **Aleesha und Sarah waren gemeinsam im Segelurlaub. Schreibe Sarahs Meinung so um, dass sie eine besondere Betonung erhalten. Aufgepasst: Manchmal musst du auch die Wortstellung ändern! Schreibe in dein Übungsheft.**

Aleesha: "Our trip to Holland was great, wasn't it? I really enjoyed it. Did you like it, too?"
Sarah: "I thought it was terrible. The weather was the worst thing (it). It was horrible (pretty). I couldn't sleep at night since it was rainy and cold (because of). And I was tired all day (really)."

Aleesha: "Oh, I didn't think it was that bad."
Sarah: "I also hated Josh's speeches (what). They were unexciting (totally)."

Aleesha: "What did you think about the food?"
Sarah: "The food was the worst thing (it). It wasn't enough for me (just)."

Aleesha: "Did you like anything at all?"
Sarah: "Well, I enjoyed being with Martin (do). He told some good jokes (really)."

Aleesha: "Well, at least you enjoyed one thing. However, I didn't like the fact that we had to go to bed at 10 p.m."
Sarah: "Right! We had to go to bed early *(vorangestellte Partizipialkonstruktion)*. This made the trip worse (even)."

Aleesha: "So, I don't think I need to ask but will you still come with us next year?"
Sarah: "I don't think so. The trip wasn't a lot of fun (no / at all)."

ÜBEN

Check-up Stil

45 Minuten

AUFGABE 1 **Benenne die Stilmittel, um die es sich hier handelt.**

Don't we all love peace and hate war? →

"All the world's a stage ..." *(William Shakespeare)* →

The dove is a ____________ for peace.

New friends. New work. New life. →

It takes two to tango. →

AUFGABE 2 **Finde einen Ausdruck, der formeller klingt.**

Thanks a lot. →

to go to school →

to quit school →

Will you be quiet. →

to take part in a discussion →

Can I use your car tomorrow? →

AUFGABE 3 **Formuliere vollständige Sätze.**

everything / Peter / prevent / drink / we / must do

Italian / suggest / learn / I

book / worth / read / be

not matter / what / say / he / nobody / listen to / him / it

more + more / earn / spend / I / money

AUFGABE 4 **Ergänze die folgenden Redewendungen mit einem der angegebenen Wörter und übersetze sie in deinem Übungsheft.**

bucket - shortest - lie - brush - pants - head - dead

to draw the ______ straw
to hit the nail on the ______
a drop in the ______
as ______ as a doornail
to have ants in your ______
A new ______ sweeps clean.
Let sleeping dogs ______.

AUFGABE 5 **Vervollständige die Sätze mit eigenen Ideen so, dass sie einen Sinn ergeben.**

No politician ______.
What I hate about ______ is that ______.
I didn't like ______. I did like, however, ______.
Being lucky, ______.

AUFGABE 6 **Übersetze und schreibe die Sätze in dein Übungsheft.**

Ich schlage vor, einen Spaziergang zu machen.
Obwohl der Koffer sehr schwer war, trug der alte Mann ihn alleine die Treppe hinauf.
Wir standen früh auf, um unseren Flug nicht zu verpassen.
Ich werde dir etwas Geld dalassen, damit du dir etwas zum Mittagessen kaufen kannst.
Ich muss alles tun, um meine Freundin davon abzuhalten, Drogen zu nehmen.
Ich wünschte, ich hätte meine Tante noch einmal besucht, bevor sie starb.
Er konnte nicht kommen, weil er krank war.

7 Umgang mit englischen Texten

7.1 Englische Texte lesen und verstehen

Texte werden unterschieden in ■ Sachtexte (1) und ■ literarische Texte (2).	(1) newspaper articles (Zeitungsartikel) – non-fictional books (Sachbücher) – advertisements (Werbetexte) – speeches (Reden) (2) poems (Gedichte) – novels (Romane) – novellas (Erzählungen) – short stories (Kurzgeschichten) – plays (Theaterstücke)
Sachtexte *(non-fictional texts)* liefern Informationen und erklären Sachverhalte. Die fünf wichtigsten Fragen an einen Text lauten: *Who? What? When? Where? Why?* Lies dir den Text gründlich durch, löse Abkürzungen auf, schlage unbekannte Wörter, Begriffe und Redewendungen nach.	**Who** reports about what? / **Who** is involved? **What** is the text about? **When** does / did the event happen? **Where** does the story take place? **Why** does something happen?And / or **why** is it important to report on?
Merke: Achte beim Lesen auf so genannte **Schlüsselbegriffe** *(keywords)* – also auf die Wörter, die den Hauptgedanken bzw. das Thema eines Texts bezeichnen.	The south-east is one of the most fascinating corners of England. Its coast and countryside are rich both in beauty and in heritage (Erbe).
Um einen **literarischen Text** *(fictional text)* zu verstehen und bearbeiten zu können, sind folgende Fragen wichtig:	
■ **Wo** und **wann** geschieht **was?**	The story itself takes place in ...
■ Wer sind die **Hauptfiguren?** Welche Eigenschaften haben sie?	The main character of the story is ... – He gives every appearance of being a well-situated, good-looking man in his forties.
■ Gibt es **Nebenfiguren?** Welchen Einfluss auf das Geschehen haben sie?	Of minor importance to the story is ...
■ Wie ist die **Beziehung** der literarischen Figuren (Charaktere) zueinander?	Among the persons in the story, XY is of special interest. – His / her attitude towards other people shows that ...
■ Was lässt sich über die **sprachliche Gestaltung** sagen?	The author uses short sentences / detailed description / few / many words to express that ... – The story is written in formal English / consists of a lot of slang expressions.

ÜBUNG 1 **Here are a couple of first lines from different types of texts. Find out which type of text these lines introduce and write down your solution.**

A Brutal Murder Two small children were among the seven victims of a bomb attack in Belfast, Northern Ireland, yesterday.	→
A busy platform. Many suitcases. An old, lonesome woman.	→
Scene I. A clearing. Thunder and lightning. Enter three witches.	→
Globalization appears to be a big issue when talking about the beginning of the 21st century.	→
Earth has not anything to show more fair: Dull would he be of soul who could pass by A sight so touching in its majesty …	→
Whether I shall turn out to be the hero of my own life, or whether that station will be held by anybody else, these pages must show. To begin my life with the beginning of my life, I record that I was born (as I have been informed and believe) on a Friday, at twelve o'clock at night.	→

ÜBUNG 2 **Match every text with a suitable headline. Be careful: One headline doesn't belong to any of the texts. Find out what kind of text this headline could match.**

A special occasion

A stairway to a better future

Old school, new methods

City Guide London

Here they are, a young couple from Mexico, a man and a woman in their early twenties, crossing borders, crossing their own borders, trying to find their way "to the promised land," trying to find, too, their way together.

London is one of the world's most vivid cities, a major business centre and capital of the United Kingdom. Among its many sights are Buckingham Palace, Hyde Park, the British Museum as well as many theatres.

By encouraging his pupils at an expensive boarding school to be brave enough to pursue their own ideas, Ron Deating, a young and ambitious teacher, runs into trouble …

ÜBUNG 3 **Read the text. Use your dictionary to look up the words in *italics*.**

Silicon Valley

Silicon Valley *is located* on the San Francisco, California, *peninsula.* At the beginning of the 20th century this area was mainly agricultural, dominated by *vast orchards.* At that time the main industries of the US were on the East Coast and California was regarded as a land of farmers. It was a wonderful sight when in spring the valley was covered with *blossoms* of many colours. Thus, it was given the name "Valley of Heart's Delight".

Everything changed in the 1930s with Fred Terman. He was a professor at Stanford University's department of electrical engineering, near San Francisco. It *troubled* him that his *graduates* could not find employment in California but had to go to the East to get a job. Fred Terman decided to make the "Valley of Delight" into the world's high-tech centre. The *US forces* were very interested in radio engineering for military reasons and, after World War II, Terman was successful in *obtaining* money for *research* from various *sources.* With this money, Terman was able to attract brilliant students and *establish* new *research departments.*

The professor did not only teach his students, but he also encouraged them to start their own companies in the valley. Two of Terman's graduates followed his *advice:* Bill Hewlett and Dave Packard. In 1939, with ideas in the field of electronics, they founded a firm, the "Hewlett-Packard Company". Their first large order was from Walt Disney Productions. It was for making motion pictures more lively. Today, Hewlett-Packard is one of the world's largest producers of computers and electronic equipment. It currently employs more than 80,000 people worldwide and has sales of more than $ 6 billion per year.

The great success of Fred Terman must also be seen from another aspect: At the age of 24, tragedy struck: he fell seriously ill with tuberculosis. Doctors gave up on him, but he *recovered.* He *suffered* all his life from his illness; at times he was able to work only two hours a day.

Despite his poor health, Terman worked with enormous energy. He built up laboratories, new university departments, and factories all at the same place. In the 1950s, he created a huge industrial park with firms like Eastman Kodak and Fairchild, the latter producing the first *semiconductors.*

In the 1980s the term "Silicon Valley" was used because the most important products, the semiconductor chips, are made of silicon. Today the former orchards have given way to the buildings of about 2000 electronics and information technology companies, including the fast-growing field of computers. Silicon Valley is the world centre of high technology.

ÜBEN

ÜBUNG 4 **What kind of text is "Silicon Valley"? Give a reason and write one or two sentences.**

ÜBUNG 5 **Now answer the following questions. Write down your answers in your exercise book.**

a) Where is Silicon Valley?
b) What could you find there at the beginning of the 20th century?
c) Where was the US industry concentrated?
d) Where did the name "Valley of Heart's Delight" come from?
e) Where did Fred Terman work?
f) What were the United States Forces interested in? Why?
g) What did Terman advise his students to do?
h) What does Hewlett-Packard produce?
i) What can you find in the industrial park which Terman created?
j) Where does the name "Silicon Valley" come from?

ÜBUNG 6 **To answer the following questions, re-read and re-think the text. Use your exercise book if necessary.**

a) Write a short characterization of Fred Terman (four to five sentences).

b) Fruit orchards versus high technology – Give at least two pros and cons for each use of the valley!

7.2 Ein *summary* schreiben

Eine **Inhaltsangabe** *(summary)* fasst die wichtigsten inhaltlichen Aussagen eines Textes zusammen. Diese werden ohne persönliche Stellungnahme der Reihenfolge nach geordnet.	
Um dem Leser eine Orientierung zu ermöglichen, wird in der **Einleitung** *(introduction)* eines *summary* das Thema formuliert und der Autor des Textes genannt.	The text by XY deals with ... – The text is a report about ... – The story is about ... – The text discusses the question if ... – The text describes / is a description of ...
Im **Hauptteil** *(main part)* des *summary* werden ■ Ort und Zeit der Handlung sowie ■ die Hauptfiguren des Textes genannt.	To begin with, the action of the story takes place in a big city / a little village ... The most important character(s) of the story is (are) ...
Diese Informationen werden geordnet: ■ Die Wiedergabe von Handlungsabläufen erfolgt entsprechend der zeitlichen Abfolge. ■ Eine Beschreibung orientiert sich an den Hauptmerkmalen.	The first part of the text explains why ... – To begin with, the author mentions that ... – Firstly / Secondly, ... – Moreover, ... – Finally / at last, ... The most important reason / argument is ... – Consequently / as a result, ...
Am Ende eines *summary* steht die **Schlussbetrachtung** *(conclusion)*. Sie fasst zusammen, mit welcher Aussage der Originaltext endet.	The text concludes by saying that ... – The author finishes by stating ...
Für die **sprachliche Gestaltung** eines *summary* gilt: ■ Sachtexte werden im *present tense* zusammengefasst: Das *past tense* wird nur verwendet, um die Vorzeitigkeit von Handlungen auszudrücken (1). ■ Verwende indirekte Rede (2). ■ Schreibe den Text nicht wörtlich ab: Verwende Synonyme und verknüpfe Aussagen mithilfe von Konjunktionen (3). ■ Teile lange Sätze und verwende Relativ- bzw. Partizipialkonstruktionen und Gerundien (↑ Kap. 4.3) (4). ■ Ersetze Aufzählungen durch Oberbegriffe (5).	(1) The article **analyses** *(present tense)* the law which **was passed** *(Vorzeitigkeit, daher past tense)* in May. (2) "Come in," said the woman. "Do you want to look at the flat?" → The woman invited him to have a look at the flat. (3) He made a lot of effort and got excellent marks in school. → As he worked hard, he earned very good results. (4) Tom is sure that he will be successful in his later school career at college. → Tom believes in succeeding at college. (5) apples, pears, bananas, cherries → fruit

ÜBUNG 7 **Read this newspaper article. Underline the most important information and keywords.**

9-year-old hands in lost cash *by Ken Parker*

A schoolgirl was praised for her honest act of handing in a bag with hundreds of pounds she had found in the street to the police in Canterbury, Kent, last week. Harriet Walker, a nine-year old girl, was on her way to a local supermarket on Saturday, April 30, when she spotted the bag with the cash.

She said, "It was so strange. I almost fell over the bag. When my foot touched it, there was the noise of coins which were clinking inside. When I opened the bag there was lots of cash. I've never seen so much money ever before." Harriet rushed back to her family's home in Canterbury, Kent, where she and her dad counted the cash before they took it to the local police station. Harriet, a primary pupil at St Martin's Primary School, said, "I'm sure it must have been someone's pension or a whole week's wage. The poor person who lost the bag must be feeling so bad now."

Parents' pride

Mr Walker, 38, who is a freelance finance consultant, said: "It was Harriet's idea to hand it in to the police. She didn't want us to tell anybody about the bag with the cash. She's such a good girl. She's our pride." Harriet's mother, 37, a housewife, said: "She's always been absolutely honest. I'm so proud of her."

Sergeant William Smith from the police station said: "Anybody who detects a purse or bag with money shows honesty when he hands it in to the police. Unfortunately, not many people do so nowadays. Harriet is a good role model for other kids. Such an act of great honesty should be praised in public because it demonstrates how to be an upright citizen."

Details about the bag or where the money was found have not been disclosed. So the owner can prove that it is theirs.

Kentish Star Monday, May 9, 2006

ÜBUNG 8 **Now look at the keywords that you've underlined. Write a list. Then sum up the main idea of the text in one sentence.**

list of key phrases:

main idea:

ÜBUNG 9 **Choose from the box below expressions that can be used instead of the ones from the text about Harriet. Form correct sentences.**

to applaud – to hurry back – to show – to see – odd

a) A schoolgirl was praised →

b) She spotted a bag. →

c) It was so strange. →

d) Harriet rushed back. →

e) It was Harriet's idea to hand it in to the police. →

f) It demonstrates how to be … →

ÜBUNG 10 **Rewrite the underlined phrases using your own words. Write into your exercise book.**

a) Harriet Walker, a nine-year-old girl, was on her way to the local supermarket when she spotted the bag with the cash.

b) She didn't want her parents to tell anybody about the bag with the cash.

c) Anybody who detects a purse or a bag with money shows honesty when he hands it in to the police.

ÜBUNG 11 **Tick off the correct answers.**

a) "I'm so sure it must have been someone's pension or a whole week's wage. The poor person who lost the bag must be feeling so bad now."

- ☐ Harriet is proud of herself that she found the money.
- ☐ Harriet pities the poor person who lost the money because she can imagine how big a loss that must be.
- ☐ Harriet envies the person who lost the money because she too wants to have a lot of money.

b) "She's always been absolutely honest. I'm so proud of her."

- ☐ Harriet's mother states that she is very pleased with her daughter.
- ☐ Harriet's mother tells the journalist that she is very disappointed in her daughter.
- ☐ Harriet's mother tells everybody that she is delighted with Harriet's behaviour.

c) "Such an act of great honesty should be praised in public because it demonstrates how to be an upright citizen."

- ☐ The sergeant thinks everybody should know that Harriet is a most honest person.
- ☐ The sergeant expresses his feelings about Harriet's honesty.
- ☐ The sergeant thinks Harriet must be seen as a perfect example for honest behaviour by everybody.

ÜBUNG 12 **Now use your list of key phrases from exercise 8 to write a summary. Remember to use synonyms and linking words and write in complete sentences. Write into your exercise book.**

7.3 Formelle Briefe schreiben

Formelle Briefe haben meist einen Betrieb bzw. eine Firma, eine Institution oder eine Behörde als Adressaten. Sie sollten die folgenden Angaben enthalten:

- vollständige Absenderangabe,
- vollständige Angabe des Adressaten,
- Datumsangabe,
- knappe Formulierung eines Betreffs,
- Anrede,
- Brieftext (auf einer neutralen bzw. formellen Sprachebene),
- Schlussformel.

BE: 5th January 2006
AE: January 5, 2006

BE: Dear Sir or Madam,
AE: Gentlemen,

BE: Yours sincerely, ...
AE: Sincerely yours, ...

Name des Adressaten nicht bekannt: Yours faithfully
vertraulicher: Yours truly, ...

Briefarten

Eine **Anfrage** *(letter of enquiry)* dient dem Zweck, genauere Informationen zu einem Produkt oder einer Dienstleistung einzuholen. Gliedere den Brief wie folgt:

- Anrede (1),
- Bezug auf die Quelle der Information (2),
- Formulierung weiterer Fragen (3),
- Schlussformel (4).

(1) Dear Mr / Mrs / Ms / Dr. Sanders, ...
(2) With reference to your advertisement in ... – On recommendation of... – We have seen from your brochure / catalogue that ...
(3) I would also like to know ... – Could you tell me whether ... – I would be grateful if you could ...
(4) Yours sincerely – Yours faithfully

Ist man mit etwas nicht zufrieden, verfasst man einen **Beschwerdebrief** *(letter of complaint)*. Er enthält:

- Angaben zu Erwerb des Produkts oder Inanspruchnahme der Dienstleistung (1),
- den Grund der Beanstandung (2),
- einen Vorschlag, wie der Schaden behoben werden kann (3),
- die höfliche Bitte um Antwort (4).

(1) + (2) Unfortunately, the product I purchased at ... on ... was damaged. ... – The goods received differ from the description in your advertisement ...
(3) I therefore suggest an exchange via one of the local dealers ...– I expect your company to compensate for my expenses ...
(4) In anticipation of your reply I remain ...

Ein **Leserbrief** *(letter to the editor / reader's letter)* zu einem in einer Zeitung veröffentlichten Beitrag enthält:

- Angaben zu dem Beitrag, auf den sich der Leserbrief bezieht (1),
- den Anlass des Schreibens (2),
- eine sachliche, neutrale Formulierung des eigenen Standpunkts (3),
- eine kurze Zusammenfassung aller wichtigen Argumente zum Schluss (4).

(1) Referring to your article "..." issued on June 5th ...
(2) I am writing to comment upon ...
(3) The most important argument, to my mind, is that ...
(4) To sum up ... – Consequently, ... – I'd like to finish saying ... – To draw a conclusion, I therefore state that ...

ÜBUNG 13 **One of the following expressions is not suitable for writing a formal letter. Cross the odd one out.**

a) Dear Madam – Hello Susan – Gentlemen – Dear Dr. Roberts

b) Please inform us about ... – Thank you for your efforts in advance. – Drop me a line. – I should be pleased to receive your answer soon.

c) Yours faithfully – Sincerely yours – Lots of love – Yours sincerely

ÜBUNG 14 **What a mess! Connect every sentence with its correct translation.**

Ich wäre Ihnen sehr verbunden, wenn Sie mir weitere Informationen zukommen lassen würden.	Please send us details concerning ...
Senden Sie uns bitte Einzelheiten über ... zu,	We have not yet received the items ordered on 11th February.
Im Voraus vielen Dank für ihre Mühe.	Thank you for your efforts in advance.
Mit Bezug auf Ihr Inserat in...	With reference to your advertisement in ...
Die am 11. Februar bestellten Produkte sind noch nicht bei uns eingegangen.	I would be grateful if you could send me further information.

ÜBUNG 15 **A letter of complaint. Fill in the gaps on this and on the following page using suitable expressions.**

11 Main Street
Canterbury
Kent EX3 5HG
(0114) 549873

5th January 2007

Customer Services
The Railroad Company
Train House
London WC5 Q7

Dear ________________,

I am writing ________________ my dissatisfaction with the poor service provided by The Railroad Company.

I am a teacher working at a Canterbury comprehensive school. Yesterday, I took my A-level students on a trip to London, __________ the 8.10 train from Canterbury to London. Not only was the train 30 min. late leaving Canterbury, but we __________ at the outskirts of London for no apparent reason. No information or __________ was offered and I still do not know the reason for our delay.
__________, as one of my students fell sick, I asked a member of the __________ to bring me a glass of water. Your staff member was most __________, telling me to go and get a glass of water myself.
__________, the many delays and troubles caused us to miss our tour guide who __________ to meet our group at Euston Station.
I had to show my students around London on my own, __________ the many interesting comments a professional guide can offer.
I am deeply convinced that you will appreciate that this level of service is __________. Thus, I expect __________ compensation for all the inconveniences and look forward to a full __________.

Yours __________,

Mary Miller

WISSEN +

Ein **Bewerbungsschreiben** *(letter of application)* enthält die folgenden Angaben:

- den Anlass der Bewerbung (1),
- bisherige Bildungsabschlüsse oder praktische Erfahrungen (Praktika, Ferienjobs) (2),
- eine Begründung der persönlichen Eignung (3),
- einen Verweis auf Anlagen *(enclosures)* (Lebenslauf, Zeugniskopien oder Empfehlungsschreiben (4),
- die Interessensbekundung an einem persönlichen Vorstellungsgespräch (5).

(1) I am writing to you with regard to your job advertisement in the *Royal Standard* of 5th Jan, 2006.
(2) I think I'm qualified for this position because I already have experience as a shop assistant.
(3) This job interests me because ...
(4) Please find my CV (curriculum vitae, *Lebenslauf*) enclosed.
(5) I would like to come to your company / your shop for a job interview. Please, contact me at ... / I am looking forward to seeing you / hearing from you.

ÜBUNG 16 Lisa Sommerfeldt wants to work as an au pair in London after leaving school in summer. However, Lisa has made a lot of mistakes. Read the letter and comment upon Lisa's mistakes. Write your comment into your exercise book.

Lisa Sommerfeldt
89230 München
Tel: (089) 789 65 43

Family Smith
33 Main Street
London W24 5LU

Application as au pair

Hello, dear Smiths,

I am a 16-year-old school girl having a lot of fun enjoying parties at the weekend. I read your ad in an old Sunday paper and since I've always wanted to live in London, I apply to stay with you.

Please tell me a possible date of arrival soon, so I can arrange a flight and pack my suitcase!

Lots of love,

Lisa Sommerfeldt

ÜBUNG 17 Improve Lisa's application. Use the following information as well as your general knowledge about how to write a letter. Write a correct letter of application into your exercise book.

Königstraße 34 – 24. März 2007 – Ihr Inserat vom 23. März 2007 – Mr and Mrs Smith – Münchner Nachrichten – Schülerin der 10. Klasse der Isar-Realschule in München – ein Bruder, 12 Jahre, Zwillingsschwestern, 9 Jahre – Vater Manager in einer Autofirma – Mutter Bankangestellte in Teilzeit – Neugierde auf den britischen Alltag – Unterricht in Kochen und Ernährungslehre seit vier Jahren

Check-up Umgang mit englischen Texten

60 Minuten

AUFGABE 1 **The missing words all have to do with texts or writing. Give the correct term.**

The end of a piece of writing is called ______________.

A person in a piece of writing, a play or a movie is a ______________.

The place where something happens is the ______________.

The most important statement in a text can be called the ______________.

An (invented) description of events and / or people is called a ______________.

AUFGABE 2 **Types of texts. Cross out the ones that don't belong.**

report – newspaper article – official invitation – novel

letter of complaint – letter of enquiry – love letter – letter of application

short story – novel – poem – election speech

AUFGABE 3 **Write five sentences which summarize the following text into your exercise book.**

Economic aspects of modern Ireland

Ireland's economy has long been dominated by agriculture. This is a thing of the past. Industry is the most important sector now, contributing 46 % to the Gross Domestic Product (GDP) *(Bruttosozialprodukt)*, almost 80 % to exports and employing close to 30 % of the labour force. Industry in Ireland is largely made up of well-known international firms, a lot of them operating in the high-tech sector. Ireland is the world's largest exporter of software and is also home to many producers of computers and computer equipment. A quarter of Europe's computers are made in Ireland by firms like Dell and IBM. One of Intel's largest and most advanced plants is located just outside Dublin. Economic growth *(wirtschaftliches Wachstum)*, however, also depends on the service industry and tourism. Tourism has a long tradition in Ireland, but today it is call centres, service operations and finance that dominate this sector. Both Apple and IBM located their European customer service operations in Ireland due to *(aufgrund)* the availability of a young, well-educated, English-speaking workforce and a good communications infrastructure. Many people calling a service hotline in Europe or the US are in fact put through to a call centre in Ireland. Ireland is no longer one of Europe's poorhouses. It has joined Europe's highly developed countries on equal terms *(hat gleichgezogen mit ...)*.

TESTEN

AUFGABE 4 Here are some useful phrases for letter writing. Complete the chart in your exercise book.

I am writing in response to your advertisement for a … in today's edition of … – On top of all this … – We have read about your product in the press. – I am currently studying … – We have seen from your brochure / catalogue that … – Please let me know … – As a consequence … – I have some experience in … – I was disappointed to find out that … – Please find enclosed a copy of … – I eagerly await your comments. – Would you please send me details of … – With reference to your advertisement in … – I am available for an interview any time. – I would appreciate if you could send me further information on/about … – It would also be helpful to know … – I expect compensation for … – Please replace the items as soon as possible. – I would be interested to know … – I am looking forward to hearing from you. – I would like a full refund.

letter of enquiry	letter of complaint	letter of application

AUFGABE 5 Write an application for a period of work experience *(Praktikumsplatz)* at the American Airlines Headquarters in New York. Use the following information to write the main body of the letter into your exercise book.

would like to collect some on-the-job experiences – Humboldt-Gymnasium, Munich, year 12 – want to improve my language skills – thank you in advance – intend to study mechanical engineering – Dear Sir or Madam – application – offer me an opportunity for work experience – from August 1st to August 31st – at your headquarters in New York – working in an English speaking country – thank you in advance for taking the trouble to read my application – enclosures: CV, copies of reports – I would be very grateful – to undertake a period of work experience

8 Englisch als Weltsprache

8.1 Britisches und amerikanisches Englisch

Die englische Sprache wird u. a. unterschieden in **britisches Englisch** *(British English, BE)* und **amerikanisches Englisch** *(American English, AE)*.

BE: taxi – *AE:* cab (Taxi)
BE: boot – *AE:* trunk (Kofferraum)
AE: I don't have any money.
BE: I haven't got any money.

British English (BE)

Britisches Englisch ist kein einheitliches Englisch, das sich überall gleich anhört. Innerhalb Englands gibt es sogar mehr Variationen des Englischen als in allen US-Staaten zusammen.
Was man normalerweise als „typisch englisch" bezeichnet, ist die *received pronunciation (RP)*, die sich an den Normen der geschriebenen Sprache orientiert.

love und luck:

im Norden Englands: [lʊv], [lʊk]

im Süden Englands: [lʌv], [lʌk]

= RP: [lʌv], [lʌk]

American English (AE)

Das Amerikanische ist sehr viel einheitlicher: Etwa zwei Drittel der Amerikaner sprechen mehr oder weniger mit dem gleichen Akzent. Dennoch gibt es auch hier regionale Unterschiede, etwa in New York.

die [daɪ], thirty-third ['θəːtɪ 'θəːd]:
A New Yorker says [dɔɪ] and ['θɔɪdɪ 'θɔɪd].

Hauptunterschiede der Aussprache

Folgende Hauptunterschiede zwischen *BE* und *AE* lassen sich feststellen:

BE:	*AE:*
"r" meist stumm	"r" ist Reibelaut,
"a" ist [ɑː]	"a" ist [æ],
"o" wird [ɔ]	"o" [ɑ],
"t" wird zu [t]	"t" wird zu [d].

door:	*BE:* [dɔː]	*AE:* [dɔːr]
dance:	*BE:* [dɑːns]	*AE:* [dæns]
hot:	*BE:* [hɔt]	*AE:* [hɑt]
butter:	*BE:* ['bʌtə(r)]	*AE:* ['bʌdər]

ÜBUNG 1 **Kennst du die amerikanische Entsprechung der britischen Begriffe?**

BE: petrol → *AE:* ______

BE: autumn → *AE:* ______

BE: mark → *AE:* ______

BE: chemist's → *AE:* ______

BE: lift → *AE:* ______

BE: headmaster → *AE:* ______

BE: lorry → *AE:* ______

BE: tap → *AE:* ______

BE: pavement → *AE:* ______

WISSEN +

Orthografische Unterschiede

Zwischen britischem und amerikanischem Englisch gibt es wichtige Unterschiede in der Schreibung:

BE: -gue	→ *AE: -g* am Wortende,	catalogue ↔ catalog; dialogue ↔ dialog
BE: -our	→ *AE: -or* am Wortende,	colour ↔ color; humour ↔ humor
BE: -ou-	→ *AE: -o-* in der Wortmitte,	mould ↔ mold; to smoulder ↔ to smolder
BE: -re	→ *AE: -er* am Wortende,	centre ↔ center; theatre ↔ theatre
BE: -ise / -isation	→ *AE: -ize / -ization* am Wortende.	recognise ↔ recognize; realisation ↔ realization

ÜBUNG 2 **Die folgenden Wörter stehen in der britischen Schreibweise. Wie werden diese im amerikanischen Englisch geschrieben?**

neighbour → ______

flavour → ______

to colonialise → ______

harbour → ______

monologue → ______

honour → ______

metre → ______

programme → ______

organisation → ______

ÜBUNG 3 **Die britische Schülerin Mary-Lou war zum Schüleraustausch in den USA. Nun schreibt sie einen Dankesbrief an ihre Gastfamilie. Unterstreiche die Begriffe, die dem amerikanischen Englisch entspringen, und schreibe die britische Entsprechung sowie die deutsche Bedeutung in deinem Übungsheft auf.**

Dear Linda,

Once again, I'd like to thank you for the wonderful time with you and your family in Michigan. I really had a wonderful time!
However, I had to acknowledge the fact that the English we speak at home is different from your language. When I told my Mum that we went on a walk with your little brother in his stroller and that we took him to the candy shop, she asked twice what we did to little Jamie ☺ ! She had also never heard about diapers and pacifiers before! On the other hand, Mum was surprised to hear that private schools are common in the States, too.
Do you remember the colorful pantyhose I bought? My friend Susan complimented me about them. Susan also really liked the purse I bought for her as a gift – as I had suspected, she went crazy for its deep green color!
Talking about friends, I especially liked the weekend we spent together with your friends staying overnight in your RV. Vacations have never been so much fun for me before!
And now I'm looking forward to the summer, when you'll come over to London! I hope you'll like it here as much as I liked it with you.

Take care,

Mary-Lou

ÜBEN

8.2 Einflüsse des Englischen auf das Deutsche

Im Deutschen finden sich zahlreiche Wörter, die aus dem Englischen entlehnt sind. Sie haben sich in ihren Lauten und Formen wie einheimische Wörter entwickelt und dem Deutschen angepasst. Solche Wörter werden als **Lehnwörter** bezeichnet.	*Lehnwörter:* *Verben:* downloaden, chatten *Partizipien:* gecheckt, recycelt
Fremdwörter dagegen erkennt man daran, dass sie mehr oder weniger unverändert ins Deutsche übernommen wurden	*Fremdwörter:* Spleen – Jeep – Hobby – Party – Sandwich – Story

Der englische Wortschatz im Deutschen

Durch die Vorreiterrolle der USA in Wirtschaft und Technik sowie durch zunehmend weltweit tätige Konzerne, die das Englische als Verkehrssprache nutzen, haben viele Begriffe Eingang ins Deutsche gefunden.	*Technik:* Computer – Spaceshuttle – Recycling – Homepage
Aber auch Begriffe aus den Bereichen Sport, Jugend und Gesellschaft stammen häufig aus dem Englischen.	*Sport:* Fan – Team – Coach – Goalkeeper *Jugend:* Freak – Teenager – Jeans *Gesellschaft:* Playboy – Gangster – Design – Highlight
Ursprünglich englische Verben werden dabei mit deutschen Vor- oder Nachsilben konjugiert.	Ich habe dir gerade eben die Bilder gemailt. Die Texte stehen zum Downloaden auf unsere Homepage bereit.
Aufgepasst: Die Verwendung von englischen Wörtern ist vor allem dann sinnvoll, wenn es im Deutschen ansonsten keinen treffenden Ausdruck gibt.	Homepage ≠ Heimatseite
Für viele englische Wörter gibt es allerdings passende deutsche Entsprechungen.	Computer = Computer *oder* Rechner

ÜBUNG 4 **Überlege, welche englischen Begriffe dir in der Alltagssprache begegnen. Nenne fünf oder sechs, die nicht auf der Wissensseite vorkommen.**

ÜBUNG 5 **Überlege dir zu den folgenden Wortfeldern je vier Beispiele englischer Begriffe, die dir in der Alltagssprache begegnen.**

Kosmetik:

Musik:

Verkehr:

Geschäftswelt:

Kultur und Medien:

ÜBUNG 6 **Lies dir den folgenden Text gründlich durch. Unterstreiche die Begriffe, die aus dem Englischen stammen, und erläutere oder übersetze sie in deinem Übungsheft.**

Im Musikbusiness werden neue Bands oft dadurch bekannt, dass sie einen Sampler zusammenstellen, auf dem sich ihr Hit befindet. Bands, die den Durchbruch schaffen, benötigen dann meist einen Manager.

Um ihr Album zu promoten, geht die Band auch auf Tour und spielt live. Bevor der Gig beginnen kann, ist ein Soundcheck erforderlich. Danach ziehen sich die Bandmitglieder meist in den Backstage-Bereich zurück, wo ihnen Dressingrooms und Catering zur Verfügung stehen. Fans haben zu diesem Bereich in der Regel keinen Zutritt, es sei denn, sie haben gute Connections und standen beim Einlass auf der VIP-Liste.

Check-up Englisch als Weltsprache

45 Minuten

AUFGABE 1 **Wie lautet die britische Entsprechung des jeweiligen amerikanischen Begriffs? Schreibe auch die deutsche Bedeutung auf.**

AE	BE	deutsche Bedeutung
chips		
cookie		
movie		
notebook		
robe		
subway		
toll-free		
trash		

AUFGABE 2 **Die folgenden Begriffe wurden falsch übersetzt. Verbessere und erkläre ihre Bedeutung.**

ACHTUNG FEHLER

the Bush administration = die Bush-Verwaltung

it doesn't make sense = es macht keinen Sinn

handyman = Handy-Spezialist

in 2007 = in 2007

Make a difference = Unterscheide dich!

TESTEN

AUFGABE 3 **Finde für die folgenden Begriffe eine passende deutsche Entsprechung oder Übersetzung.**

Public Relations →

canceln →

Snack →

Casting →

Shootingstar →

Feedback →

Meeting →

Website →

Callcenter →

AUFGABE 4 **Jeff aus Kalifornien macht während der Sommerferien ein dreiwöchiges Praktikum in einem Reisebüro in London. Er berät ein Ehepaar, das seine Reiseunterlagen abholt. Fülle die britische Entsprechung des jeweiligen Begriffs in die Lücken.**

Jeff: "Here are your travel vouchers: your plane tickets, some hotel addresses and – very important – some immigration forms. Please note that you've got to fill out these forms before you clear customs."

Mrs Green: "So we've got to ______ some forms? Well, we'll manage."

Jeff: "As soon as you've arrived at the airport, transportation to your hotel is really easy. Take a shuttle from the airport to the hotel, hand your baggage to the bellboy and check in at the reception."

Mrs Green: "You mean we shall hand our ______ to the ______? Never! I don't trust anybody than myself!"

Jeff: "I'm sorry. You don't have to do that. But it would make things easier for you."

Mrs Green: "We are not that old!"

Jeff: "And as a little gift from the travel agency, here are two daypacks with the company logo. Have a wonderful vacation!"

Mrs Green: "Well, we've never used ______ before. But thank you very much for the ______. We are really excited and we are looking forward to our ______."

TESTEN

1 Die Zeiten

Ü1 After a long day at school, Laura **comes** home, **throws** her school bag into the corner and **walks** into the kitchen. Her mother **is cooking** dinner.

Laura: "Hi, Mum! Oh, you **are not preparing** potato soup again, are you?"

Mother: "Potato soup? Of course, Laura! Whenever I **cook,** I always **cook** soup or stew. You should **know** that I can't **cook** anything else."

Laura: "Oh Mum, you **are teasing.** You **know** very well how much I **love** your lasagne."

Mother: "Yes, I **know.** But lasagne always **is** a lot of work, and I came home from work only fifteen minutes ago. Listen! The phone **is ringing.** Can you **answer** it, please?"

Laura **walks** into the living room and **picks up** the phone. She is **still talking** to her friend when her Dad **walks** into the house.

Dad: "Hello everybody!"

Mother: "Hello, Peter. Laura **is** in the living room."

Dad: "Oh Laura, you're crazy! Whenever I **come** home from work, you **are talking** on the phone. Listen! Mother **is calling.** Dinner **is** ready."

Laura **says** good-bye to her friend on the phone, **replaces** the receiver and **walks** into the kitchen. The whole family **is eating** dinner. But soon enough, the phone **is ringing** again ...

Ü2 a) Our teacher always **forgets** his book. →
Unser Lehrer **vergisst immer** sein Buch.
I **am forgetting** my French. →
Ich **vergesse allmählich** mein Französisch.
b) This vine **tastes** awful. →
Der Wein **schmeckt** scheußlich.
She **is tasting** red vine with some chocolates. →
Sie **probiert** Rotwein mit Schokolade.
c) She **wants** to become a teacher. →
Sie **will** Lehrerin werden.
Their daughter **is wanting** in good manners. →
Ihre Tochter **lässt** gute Manieren vermissen.
d) She **is seeing** a psychiatrist. →
Sie **geht zu** einem Psychiater.
He always **sees** his daughter on Sundays. →
Er **trifft** seine Tochter immer sonntags
e) I'm thinking of going to London. →
Ich denke darüber nach, nach London zu fahren.
I **think** he's right. → Ich **glaube,** dass er Recht hat.

Ü3

infinitive	simple past	deutsche Bedeutung
to catch	caught	fangen, erreichen
to lie	lay	liegen
to win	won	gewinnen
to throw	threw	werfen
to become	became	werden
to fall	fell	fallen
to show	showed	zeigen
to read	read	lesen

Ü4 My big sister was preparing dinner when the electricity went off.
Laura was playing the violin when the telephone rang.
Father was dusting the cupboard when the match between Liverpool and Manchester ended.
The shop assistant was trying on an expensive dress when her boss came in.
The taxi driver was parking in a handicapped parking space when the police drove by.
When my friends and I were walking home, it started to rain.

Ü5 Last summer I **had** a very frightening experience. At that time I **was travelling** the United States. I used to **put up** my tent quite regularly in one of the many National Parks, and I always **slept** very well. One night, however, at about 9 o'clock at night, while I **was reading** a book by the flickering light of my torch, I **heard** somebody scream. I **closed** my book and **turned** my flashlight off. I **was** just **lacing up** my shoes when I **heard** a terrible snort.

Something enormous **was standing** in front of my tent! I **did not dare** to breathe. "That might be a bear," I **thought.** Then I **remembered** my whistle. I **blew** the whistle and the bear **disappeared.** I **was** still **trembling** when I turned my flashlight on again and I **did not sleep** well that night.

Next morning, when I **went** into the next village to do some shopping, I **asked** a ranger about bears in national parks. He **told** me that there had been no bear around at all the previous night.

I **trembled** again: **Was** I **having** a dream when I **heard** the screaming and snorting last night?

Ü6 Grandfather worked three hours in the garden yesterday afternoon.
The taxi driver didn't know the city at all.
Jill was just doing her homework when her boyfriend came to visit.
Our maths teacher wasn't nice at all today.
Where were you when it started / began to snow?

Ü7

infinitive	past participle	deutsche Bedeutung
to sell	sold	verkaufen
to rise	risen	steigen, aufgehen
to put	put	legen, stellen
to bite	bitten	beißen
to grow	grown	wachsen
to know	known	wissen, kennen
to begin	begun	anfangen
to draw	drawn	zeichnen

Ü8 I **have always dreamt** of having a pet.
It's 10 p.m. already. How long **have you been watching** TV?
My parents **have never been** to China.
I'm exhausted. I **have been cleaning** the house since 8 o'clock this morning.
Look at this mess! I **have dropped** my bag.

Ü9 Hanna has been playing the piano since she was six years old.
We have been preparing a dinner party since 4 p.m.
My dad has had his computer since 1990.
Amy and Evan have owned their house for six years now.
Petra has sent me a postcard every week since she moved here.

Ü10 Our school has had a new headmaster since the beginning of the year.
A lot has changed since January.
For how long have you been looking for your earring?
The Millers haven't sold their old car yet.
Ben has already eaten two chocolate bars today.

Ü11 Yesterday, Evan **got up** early and **took** his kids to the zoo. Maya **enjoyed** watching the penguins, and Milo **had** a lot of fun feeding the ducks. After a picnic lunch, Evan **bought** the kids an ice cream. Maya and Milo **were running** around the zoo happily for many hours and **had** a perfect day.
At home, Evan's wife Amy **had** a wonderful day, too. She **enjoyed** the quietness. She **took** a bath. She **read** a book and **took** a nap in the sunshine. And after so many hours to herself, she **was looking forward to** seeing her family again.
Rückwärts erzählt:
Yesterday, after many hours to herself, Amy had been looking forward to seeing her family again. She had had a wonderful day at home and had enjoyed the quietness. She had taken a bath, read a book and taken a nap in the sunshine. Amy's husband Evan had gotten up early and had taken the kids to the zoo. Maya had enjoyed watching the penguins, and Milo had had a lot of fun feeding the ducks. After a picnic lunch, Evan had bought the kids an ice cream. Maya and Milo had been running around the zoo for many hours. They had had a perfect day, too.

Ü12 After Sam and Sarah had decided to marry, they sent out invitation cards.
After they had sent out invitation cards, they looked around for a nice party location.
After Sarah and Sam had decided on a meal, they went shopping for a wedding dress and a suit.
After they had had everything ready, Sam and Sarah panicked: the idea of having such a big party was simply too much for them.
After they had said sorry to all their friends, they flew to the Caribbean Sea.
After they had gotten married on the beach of a romantic island, they had a wonderful honeymoon.

Ü13 Many years ago, while I **was living** in New Zealand, I once **went** whale-watching on a small boat.
I **have been** to London twice already.
Sarah **was** late for lunch because she **had missed** the school bus.
We **spent** our holidays in Africa last summer.
When I **was** a little girl, my sister and I **quarrelled** many times a day.
Kim **has visited** her friend in hospital twice since last Sunday.
We always **have** cereal for breakfast.
Her brother came home while Laura **was ringing** a friend.
I **am** a teacher. I **taught** our former president while he **was attending** the local school. I **have known** him ever since.
While Luke and Anna **were kissing** on the bench in the park, someone **broke** into their car and **stole** all their money.
Last Christmas, I **got** a new bike.

I **was** in the hospital last summer because I **had broken** my leg.
Carolyn **loves** cherries. Every summer, she **goes** to the supermarket and **buys** at least one pound of cherries.
Paul **has never been** to Germany. He **wanted** to go last spring but he **was** out of money and **couldn't** afford to go.

Ü14

infinitive	will-future	future progressive	future perfect
to go	will go	will be going	will have gone
to catch	will catch	will be catching	will have caught
to talk	will talk	will be talking	will have talked
to speak	will speak	will be speaking	will have spoken
to write	will write	will be writing	will have written

Ü15 Tim, you **are going to write** a math exam next Thursday. **Don't forget** to study!
Rose, there **is** a concert scheduled for you to play on Wednesday. Please promise that you **will practise** every day. And don't forget to ask Sarah whether her Mom or Dad **will be able to** take you home. And don't forget your friend's birthday tomorrow. Lisa's mother told me that they **are going to take** you all to the cinema.
Peter, we've invited friends for a barbecue the very evening of my return. You **will have to do** the shopping. And you **will be spending** that afternoon cleaning up the backyard, okay?
I've got to hurry now. My train **leaves** at 7.15 a.m. Have a good time. Bye!

Ü16 *Michael:* "I am **not going to study** any vocabulary over the holidays. However, I **will be staying** with my girlfriend at her aunt's for one week. And as soon as I **will have finished** school next summer, I **will take** my girlfriend on a trip round the world."
Sarah: "I hope it **will be** hot all summer. Then I'**ll be spending** every afternoon at the swimming-pool. I assume I'**ll get** a good tan then."
Mary: "I **am going to sleep in** every day. And I'**m going to do** a lot of shopping in our shopping centre."
Susie: "My parents and I **are going to spend** two weeks in Greece. I guess we'**ll do** a lot of sight-seeing there."
Sharif: "I'**m going to redecorate** my room. Maybe I'**ll make** a new shelf. I hope I'**ll have finished** all the work until school starts again."
Monica: "We **will be hosting** an exchange student from New Zealand. She'**ll be arriving** at London Airport next Saturday. And I **am going to visit** her in New Zealand over Christmas."
Marc: "I **won't do** anything special. I'**ll just relax and see** what happens."
Teacher: "I hope you'**ll enjoy** your holidays. Relax – you'll need a lot of strength as soon as school **starts** again on September 1st."

Ü17 Don't eat that chocolate now. We **are about to** have lunch in a minute.
Kate has got good nerves. I **expect her to** pass the driving test easily.
Stop teasing your little sister. Look at her, she **is about to** cry!
Your exam results are terrible. I **wish to** speak to your teacher as soon as possible.

Ü18 *Mary:* "Are you coming / going to come to our schoolparty tonight, Kate? Peter and Marc are going to come / will be coming, too, and I think the party will be really good."
Kate: "I'm sorry, I won't make it / I'm not going to make it to the party tonight. I've promised to babysit my little sister. If I don't do it, there will be trouble."
Mary: "What time will your parents be home again?"
Kate: "I don't know. Maybe at around 10 o'clock at night?"
Mary: "The party will certainly be going on much longer. Why don't you show up later?"
Kate: "All right. I'll come as soon as my parents are back home again."
Mary: "Great! I'm looking forward to tonight! Bye, Kate!"
Kate: "See you!"

Ü19 Look, the sun **is coming out.**
Paris Hilton **had been walking** around London with her huge sunglasses for three hours before anybody recognized her.
Since 2003, my sister **has been living** in New Zealand.
I usually get up at 6.30 but today I **am staying** in bed.
While my father **was digging** a hole for the gas pipe, he listened to the radio.

Ü20 Next year my husband and I **will have been married** for ten long and endless years.
Don't worry. The plane **won't have left** before we get to the airport.

Next summer I **will have worked** in the same boring job with the same company for over eight years.

Ü21 Since his wife left him, Peter **has been cooking** his own dinner.
Mickie **has been practising** karate for two hours now.
Last night, Ashley **didn't drink** any beer. Do you think she **is** pregnant?
When you came in with that fancy dress, you **looked** like a hippie from the sixties.
I was sick because I **had eaten** to many scoops of ice cream.
It **had been raining** all day when Sarah **remembered** that she **forgot** to take the laundry inside.

Ü22 *Lea:* "**Will you go out** to the party with us next Friday night?"
Hannah: "No, I won't. **I'm going to meet** a guy named Johnny."
Lea: "What **will you be doing** all night?"
Hannah: "We probably **will be having** dinner first. And later we **will go** dancing."
Lea: "Do you think you **will enjoy** spending time with a boy you've never met before?"
Hannah: "Well, I hope it **won't be** boring."

Ü23 He came into the living room while I **was watching** TV.
What are you doing at the moment? – I **am preparing** dinner.
Two years ago, while I **was travelling** through Spain, I **met** the man who now **is** my husband.
She has **not read** a book since her baby daughter **was** born last January.
When my grandmother **was** a little girl, she **was living** in Hungary.
Yesterday, Annie was late for work because her son **had fallen** sick.
Our plane to Los Angeles **leaves** Frankfurt Airport at 10 o'clock next Monday.
Next January, they **will have been married** for 15 years.
Kate **has visited** her brother three times since he is in hospital.
Carla used **to be** a good pupil. However, she **fell** seriously sick last winter and **has missed** a lot of lessons, so she now has a hard time catching up in all the topics.

Check-up Kapitel 1

A1 we / think *(present perfect simple)* → **we have thought**
I / learn / past *(past perfect progressive)* → **I had been learning**
you / put *(will-future)* → **you will put**
he / carry *(simple present)* → **he carries**
she / begin *(future perfect)* → **she will have begun**
it / bring *(simple past)* → **we brought**
we / overtake *(present progressive)* → **we are overtaking**
you / go *(going to-future)* → **you are going to go**
we / laugh *(past progressive)* → **we were laughing**
he / speak *(past perfect simple)* → **he had spoken**
it / rain *(future progressive)* → **it will be raining**

A2 It **is** summer. The sun **is shining** and it **is getting** really hot. Sarah **is** on the beach. She **is writing** a postcard.

Dear Sally,
I **am writing** these lines on the beach. We usually **spend** our holiday in Great Britain, but it **rains** a lot there. So this year we **are spending** our holidays in Spain.
At the moment, I **am enjoying** the sun, the beach and the ocean. But I **don't like** our hotel: The meals **taste** awful and my bed **smells** of cat droppings.
Lots of love,
Sarah

A3 We **went** to Greece two years ago.
This room **smells** terribly. Close the door, please.
Before Mary **went** out for dinner with her boyfriend, she **had done** all her homework, had called her friend, **had decided** what to wear and **had taken** a shower.
Why **didn't you come** to Sarah's party last night? – I **had** a bad headache so I **thought** I'd better stay at home.
As a young woman, my Mom used to **play** the guitar.
Be quiet, please. I **am listening** to my favourite song.
"What **were you doing** at 10 p.m. last night?" my mother **asked** at breakfast.
The Beatles **wrote** numerous songs.

A4 Kate **has been** at school **since** 8 o'clock this morning.
My friends **have been living** in San Francisco **for** six years now.
I'm awfully cold. I **have been waiting** for the train to arrive **for** half an hour.

Liz **has not studied** her vocabulary **for** many weeks. Tomorrow's French test will be very difficult for her.
My parents **have known** each other **for** 20 years.
Laura and Hanna **have been** friends **since** 2002.
Kim **has been reading** that novel **for** a long time.
Janet and Sarah **have been talking** on the phone for more than one hour now.

A5 At eight o'clock tonight, this shop **will be** closed.
She **won't be coming** any more. It's too late now.
Sarah's parents argue all day. I guess they **are going to split up.**
My sister is pregnant. I hope she **will marry** soon.
We've just bought a big property. By next October, we **will be living** in our own house.
The fog **will clear** up soon.
She **is giving** a party together with her best friend.
This summer holiday, I **will be staying** at my aunt's in Australia.
My family **is going to go** to Spain this summer.
Will you have finished your homework by 5 o'clock this afternoon?

A6 Lösungsvorschlag:
After I got dressed for the evening, I met my friend Sarah at the bus stop. We took the bus to get to Peter's house. After we had greeted Peter's parents, who were watching a TV show in the living room, we went downstairs. All our friends were there already. And after Peter's mother had come down to serve some snacks, the party wasn't interrupted again by adults. We played some party games and danced a lot. I haven't had such a great evening for a long time.

A7 The mechanic won't have repaired the dishwasher by Monday.
What will we be doing at this time next year?
They are getting married in May.
I broke my leg last week.
Laura has been doing her homework for three hours.
When does the next train leave for London?
A lot has changed in her / their company lately.

2 Das Passiv

Ü1 to catch *(present perfect simple)* → **have / has been caught**
to choose *(simple past)* → **was / were chosen**
to give *(will-future)* → **will be given**
to carry *(simple present)* → **am / is / are carried**
to ask *(past perfect)* → **had been asked**
to hold *(simple past)* → **was / were held**
to wake up *(present perfect simple)* → **have / has been woken up**

Ü2 Lösungsvorschlag:
a) The dog is being washed.
Last Thursday, the dog was washed / was being washed.
The dog has been washed for half an hour.
b) A bank is being robbed.
At 10 o'clock yesterday, a bank was robbed / was being robbed.
The bank has never been robbed.
c) The house is being painted.
Next spring, the house will be painted.
The house was painted / was being painted last summer.

Ü3 Traveller cheques are accepted (by this restaurant).
Japanese isn't taught by many teachers.
The boat was destroyed by the storm.
A bear has been seen in the forest (by someone).
Paul is loved by everybody.

Ü4 The old lady's shopping has been done and she walks home slowly. Secretly, she is followed by a young man. As soon as the door of her apartment has been unlocked, the old lady is knocked down. The apartment is entered by the criminal, every single room is looked through and all valuables are taken away.
Fifteen minutes later, the old lady is discovered in the corridor by a neighbour. The police are called. The old lady is taken to hospital by the paramedics. A week later, the thief is caught in a traffic check: He was driving too fast.

Ü5 Last year, the old lady's shopping had been done and she walked home slowly. Secretly, she was followed by a young man. As soon as the door of her apartment had been unlocked, the old lady was knocked down. The apartment was entered by the criminal, every single room was looked through and all valuables were taken away.
Fifteen minutes later, the old lady was discovered in the corridor by a neighbour. The police were called. The old lady was taken to hospital by the

paramedics. A week later, the man was caught in a traffic check. He was driving too fast.

Ü6 I was told the news by my friend. / The news were told to me by my friend.
A new pair of jeans was bought for Laura. / Laura was bought a new pair of jeans.
Meggie was read a book by her grandmother. / A book was read to Meggie by her grandmother.
A birthday present was given to his girlfriend by Peter. / His girlfriend was given a birthday present by Peter.

Ü7 Lösungsvorschlag:
Yesterday, a meeting was held at 3 p.m. to organize our school party in July. The date of the school party, which will be July 8th, had been fixed two days ago by the headmaster. During the meeting, a lot of different subjects were discussed, such as food, drinks and games. At the end, a date for the next meeting was fixed.
It will be held June 8th at 3 p.m. Help is needed, so come and join the party team!

Ü8 The staff **ought to be informed** about all changes in every patient's condition.
The patients **can be visited / are allowed to be visited** from 10 a.m. until 5 p.m.
All medicine **must be locked away / has to be locked away** in the nurses' office.
All documents should be handled confidentially.
Just in case: Forgotten items **are to be taken** to the nurses' office.

Ü9 Lösungsvorschlag:
Jimmy was made fun of last Saturday.
The baby is always looked after.
The new houses are being looked at at the moment.
The speech was listened to two days ago.
This apartment building will be pulled down next month.
This bank has never been broken into.

Ü10 Tom **is said / reported / believed to be** very sensitive.
The president didn't appear for the talk show. **It is said / reported / believed** that he couldn't come because he is quite ill.
Thousands of children **are said / reported / believed** to have lost a close relative in the earthquake in Asia last December.
Last night, a terrible accident happened on the motorway to London. **It is said / reported / believed that** four people were killed.

Ü11 All rules must be followed / are to be followed by the team.
Her dad is said to be a rich man.
Hanna was asked many questions by her teacher.
The neighbour is being taken to hospital.
I hope I will be offered a good job next year.
When I came home from school last week, our car was being hauled away.

Check-up Kapitel 2

A1 to tell *(present perfect simple)* → **has / have been told**
to spend *(simple past)* → **was / were spent**
to bite *(will-future)* → **will be bitten**
must find *(simple present)* → **must be found**
to drive *(past perfect simple)* → **had been driven**
to keep *(simple past)* → **was / were kept**
to sing *(present perfect simple)* → **has / have been sung**

A2 Hanna is allowed to eat an ice cream.
She is taken to the playground.
Hanna's mum is called and told how nice Hanna is.
Hanna is sent to bed very early.

A3 Lea's dog is being taken for a walk.
Look! The car is being washed.
The fish in the pond weren't fed / were not fed by Tom.
Her purse had been stolen by somebody.
Many years ago in first grade, we were taught the alphabet.
Books are often given away by my mother.
I haven't been given a birthday present by my friends so far.

A4 The wallpaper **was being taken down** when the phone rang.
A party **was being held** when a heavy thunderstorm struck.
An exam **was being written** when the fire alarm was set off.

A5 Some cars **are made** with a lot of plastic.
These flowers are really dry. They **must be watered** by somebody.
A century ago, most books **were read** by more than one reader. Today, a lot of books **are never read** by anybody.
Look! Brad Pitt **is being filmed** over there!
The first automobile **was invented** by Karl Benz in 1885.

A6 As a baby, life is very easy. Babies are fed about five times a day and are entertained. And in a lot of families, the baby is spoilt by the grandparents, too. For example, it is taken for a walk in its pushchair. Yes, it's true – babies lead an easy life.
Lösungsvorschlag:
But as a teenager, life changes. As we all know, we usually have to look after ourselves. At least, our meals are still often cooked for us, and our laundry is washed together with all the dirty clothes of the whole family. But all our homework has to be done by ourselves, and our rooms have to be kept tidy. And very often there are more jobs for us to do: Some money has to be earned, friends have to be met, little brothers and sisters have to be kept out of the way – well, as a teenager, life isn't as easy as before.

3 Die indirekte Rede

Ü1 sagen → **to say;** fragen → **to ask;** erzählen, sagen → **to tell;** denken → **to think;** berichten (über) → **to report;** erwähnen → **to mention;** etwas wissen wollen / gespannt sein → **to wonder**
Merksatz: Alle diese Verben können einen Satz in indirekter Rede einleiten. Es handelt sich um *einleitende Verben,* englisch *reporting verbs.*

Ü2 Tim said that that **was** an unbelievable story.
Marc states that in his opinion accounting **is** a boring job for boring people.
Kate told her friend that if she **ever married,** she **would only marry** someone rich.
Sarah said that her grandfather **had become** less active during the past months. She added that she **hoped** he **would not** die soon.

Ü3 Susi told her teacher that she was sorry that she hadn't understood his explanation and that she hadn't done her homework.
Lisa asked whether I / he / she / we / they had ever heard about the terrible famine in Ireland in the early 19th century.
Tom said that he had had a bad day yesterday, that he had missed his bus, had been late for school and had lost his watch on the way home.

Ü4 The Millers say that they go out for dinner once a week.
The teacher asked his pupils whether / if they liked reading.
Susan says that she hasn't studied her English vocabulary in a while. And she adds that they will be writing a test the next week, so she had better study them that night.
Lucy told her friend that she had met a nice boy at the disco the night before / the previous night.
The teacher said that they would go on a one-week school trip to London the following March.
Laura said that she had never been to San Francisco before. And she added that her younger sister had travelled to San Francisco the previous May.
Laura states that Melanie's party starts at 7.30 p.m. tonight.
Rob says that he'll buy a new mobile phone the next month.
Anne told Mary that she had met their maths teacher at that Italian pizza place the day before / the previous day.
Cynthia told her boyfriend that it was her Chinese grandma's birthday that day and that she was going to celebrate there in England.
Aunt Helen asked where my mother had gone because she hadn't seen her that day.

Ü5 Simon: "This morning at school, the teacher told us that we would be leaving for London the following Saturday and that our train would leave *(timetable future: would + infinitive!)* the station at 9.15 a.m. She added that latecomers who would miss that train would not be able to participate in the trip at all. Nobody was going to wait for them. And she said that alcohol was forbidden on the whole trip and that pupils drinking alcohol would be sent home at their own expense. Then she said that he was looking forward to our trip and that she was sure it would be fun."

Ü6 Journalists ~~believed~~ **believe** that more newspapers are sold at weekends when you have enough time to sit and read for hours.
Today it is widely accepted that Canadian Inuit and Indians ~~were~~ **are** proud of having been their country's first inhabitants.
It is said that Christopher Columbus discovered America ~~in 1692~~ **in 1492.**
My mother ~~said~~ **said to me / told me** that most TV programmes ~~are~~ **were** not really worth watching.
The girl said that she was just eating chocolate. → ***richtig***
It is said that in Shakespearean times women ~~had~~ **were** not allowed to perform on stage.

Ü7 **a)** <u>shall</u> / will / may
b) can / <u>must</u> / will
c) <u>ought to</u> / may / can

Ü8 Gary asked whether / if we should go out for dinner the following Saturday.
Mother said (that) I mustn't / shouldn't / wasn't to eat so much chocolate.
The bank manager said (that) I had to pay back the money that month.
Peter told Kate that she must be tired after running the marathon. (**Merke:** *must* bleibt unverändert, da es sich um eine Annahme bzw. Schlussfolgerung handelt!)
The teacher said that I needn't / didn't have to worry about my school report.
Tom said that he was sure he would enjoy his holidays.
The coach said that he might need some help with the junior team.
The sign said that you mustn't / weren't to eat ice cream while riding the tram.

Ü9 Mary asked Jodie where she had met her boyfriend for the first time.
Michael asked Tom if / whether he had ever been to Los Angeles.
Jasmin asked Maggie if / whether she had seen Mrs Miller's new glasses. She added that they looked very expensive.
Daneesh asked Peter whether / if he would come to Mike's party the following weekend.

Ü10 Lösungsvorschlag:
Anne promised to buy me a new book.
Amy warned me not to eat too many chillis because they were very hot.
Father threatened to take away my computer if I didn't pass my exam.
My older sister told me / asked me to lay the table.

Ü11 Jane said that Peter was bad at biology.
My parents say that they will be home late.
Vicky said that she felt sick.
Theresa told Marco that they had written a maths exam.
My mother wanted to know where the party would take place.
She asked me whether I would go shopping with her.

Check-up Kapitel 3

A1

direkte Rede		indirekte Rede
past progressive	→	***past perfect progressive***
could	→	***could***
present tense	→	*past tense*
goingto-future	→	***was / were going to + infinitive***
will-future	→	*would + infinitive*
mustn't	→	***mustn't / shouldn't / wasn't to / weren't to***
needn't	→	*didn't have to*

A2 Nikos said that he **hadn't seen** his Greek relatives for ages.
Sue says that she **is going to play** chess all day.
Morris stated that he **would be enjoying** his work even at age 85.
Peter wanted to know where we **had been** the night before.

A3 We promise / are told to be polite to all guests within the premises.
We promise / are told not to insult other people.
We promise / are told not to fight with other party guests.
We promise / are told to help our fellows when necessary.
We promise / are told not to drink and drive.

A4 Charles said he thought he knew that book.
Megan says that she hasn't had an ice cream for a while.
Michelle told Anne that her friend from Germany would be visiting in July.
Tom said that his father had gone on a hike which he had often done before.
Laura wanted to know whether / if her little sister had seen their rabbit somewhere lately.
Rachel said that she hadn't gone to her piano lesson that afternoon because she had felt sick.
Mother told Lily that she wasn't allowed to go to the party that night.
Amy asked Leo whether / if they would see each other the following year.
James told us that he was just preparing lunch.

A5 Melanie advised me to see a doctor.
My aunt wanted to know if / whether we would come over for lunch next Sunday.
She complained that she had very few books to read.

Cara said that she had moved into her house in 2004.
Ken wanted to know which team had won the match.
The mother told the kids to tidy up their room.
The teacher told his pupils that they would go on an excursion the following day.
She said she had lived in China for three years.

4 Der Satz

Ü1 wenn, falls → **if;** vorausgesetzt, dass → **provided that;** es sei denn → **unless;** angenommen, dass → **supposing that**
Merksatz: Alle diese Wörter sind Konjunktionen, die einen Bedingungssatz einleiten können.

Ü2 a) Typ II
b) Typ I
c) Typ I
d) Typ II
e) Typ III

Ü3 Es handelt sich um einen Bedingungssatz des Typs I, auch wenn im Hauptsatz kein *will-future*, sondern das *simple present* steht. Das *simple present* bedeutet hier nämlich, dass etwas (also das Öffnen der Tür) eine automatische Folge (des Knopfdrehens) ist, die immer wieder passiert.

Ü4 No. If Laura studied Spanish with her Dad, they would quarrel soon.
No. If Mary worked at the airport, she would have to be able to speak more languages.
If I had spent the night with my friends, I would not have been able to go to school the next day.

Ü5 a) If you try our super sweet chocolate, you will never forget the taste.
If you tried our super sweet chocolate, you would never forget the taste.
If you had tried our super sweet chocolate, you would have never forgotten the taste.
b) If you don't drink and drive, you will be safe.
If you didn't drink and drive, you would be safe.
If you hadn't drunk and driven, you would have been safe.
c) If you hike New Zealand, you will enjoy the wilderness.
If you hiked New Zealand, you would enjoy the wilderness.
If you had hiked New Zealand, you would have enjoyed the wilderness.
d) If you colour your life with Wonder-Colour, you will feel better.
If you coloured your life with Wonder-Colour, you would feel better.
If you had coloured your life with Wonder-Colour, you would have felt better.

Ü6 If I travel to Los Angeles, I will visit Hollywood.
If you saw the Louvre, you would know you were in Paris.
If you had seen the Berlin wall in the 80s, you would have felt uneasy.
If you protested against lower wages, you would get fired.
If she comes to Athens one day, she will walk up the hill to visit the Acropolis.
If I had read that travel book, I would have known that the museum was closed on Wednesdays.

Ü7 If I had passed the exam, my Dad would not have been upset.
Can we build a snowman tomorrow if it snows?
My friend would not have broken her leg if she had stayed at home over the holidays.
If the company was sold, a lot of employees would become jobless.

Ü8 My aunt Pam**, who** had given me a ticket for the *Pink* concert**,** went to see the show, too. The tram **that / which** we took to get to the arena was loaded with young people **who** were talking about pop stars and rock concerts. At the entrance my aunt met a friend **who / that** she hadn't seen in a while. She**, who** usually doesn't talk a lot**,** couldn't stop chatting. She told her friend**, who** had travelled 400 km to come to the concert**,** the story of her life and vice versa. And guess what? My aunt's friend knew someone from the concert crew and had got backstage passes! So at the end, my aunt and I got backstage passes, too! My aunt**, who** was even more excited than I was**,** made my day: I talked to *Pink* herself! It's unbelievable, isn't it?

Ü9 My Dad, who likes to eat, cooked this wonderful meal.
Madame Monique, who is our French teacher, is married to a physician.
The book (which) I found on the underground is boring. → *contact clause!*
My boyfriend, who I like very much, gave me tickets for the pop concert.
The boy (who is) talking to Jane is her brother. → *contact clause!*
Ronald Reagan, who was also president of the USA, was a movie star.

Ü10 A hotel is a building which is built for travellers.
A dog is an animal which / that can be a good friend.
A fairy is a creature that does magic.
Ireland is a country which / that has a shamrock as symbol.
An old castle is a building that attracts visitors.
A bus is a means of transportation which / that can transport a group of people.

Ü11 That's the tram ~~who~~ → **which / that *(oder contact clause)*** I usually take.
Where is the girl ~~whom~~ → **who / that** wants to become a movie star?
That's the boy ~~that~~ → **whose** mother is Italian.
Is this the magazine ~~who~~ → **which / that *(oder contact clause)*** you were talking about?
Brazil is not the only country ~~who~~ → **which / that** has a good football team.
My Dad and I saw our favourite football team win, ~~that~~ → **which** made us very happy.

Ü12 The house which / that belongs to Mary's parents looks like / resembles a palace.
Is he the boy who can ride a unicycle?
Is that the girl whose parents are both doctors?
People who smoke can damage their health.
Money (that / which) is spent on education is a good investment.

Ü13 How about to travel to Hawaii next summer? → ***wrong:*** How about **travelling** to Hawaii ...?
There must be a reason for cooking potatoes. → ***right***
Ian spent a lot of time to try to find a birthday present for his girlfriend.→ ***wrong:*** Ian spent a lot of time **trying** to find a birthday present ...
He hates living in the countryside.→ ***right***
He hates to live in the city. → ***right***
This morning, she left the house without to eat breakfast.→ ***wrong:*** This morning she left the house without **eating** breakfast.

Ü14 My parents don't allow me **to watch** TV late at night.
I wondered what **to buy** for her birthday.
How about **eating out** tonight?
She has a lot of experience **in teaching.**
She opened the window in order **to let** some fresh air in.
My brother loves **to hike / hiking** in the Alps.
The pupils concentrate on **writing** their exam.

Ü15 **a)** My boyfriend stopped smoking. (he stopped to smoke = er blieb stehen, um zu rauchen)
b) He used to get up early. (he is used to getting up early = er ist es gewöhnt, früh aufzustehen)
c) We tried to find the keys. (we tried finding the keys = wir probierten aus, die Schlüssel zu finden)
d) Letzten Winter habe ich Snowboarden ausprobiert. (I tried to snowboard = ich habe versucht zu snowboarden)
e) I must remember to buy some tea. (I must remember buying some tea = ich muss daran denken, wie ich Tee gekauft habe)
f) You forgot meeting Jill, didn't you? (you forgot to meet Jill = du hast vergessen, sie zu treffen)

Ü16 **Buying a novel** at her favourite bookstore, Jane noticed that one of the customers was watching her closely. But **having made up** her mind, Jane was determined to buy that book. **Throwing** a glance at that customer, she went to the cashier's desk. He was getting ready to walk up to the cashier's desk, too. **Having paid for** the book, Jane was walking out onto the street. **Following her,** the young man called after her. **Excusing himself,** he asked Jane why she had bought the book. Jane answered that a good friend had recommended it to her. **Thanking** Jane, the young man said that he was the author of this book.

Check-up Kapitel 4

A1 **allow:** Das Verb *to allow* verlangt kein Gerundium.
typical of: Die anderen drei Ausdrücke sind Substantive, auf die das Gerundium folgt, *typical of* ist jedoch ein Adjektiv, auf das ein Substantiv folgt *(red vine is typical of that region).*
to detest: Das Verb *to detest* verlangt das Gerundium, die anderen drei Verben den Infinitiv.

A2 They have been dreaming **of / about** buying a house since 1998.
My parents have an interest **in** gardening.
Most immigrants have difficulties **in** finding a good job.
My brother must have a reason **for** being so helpful with the dishes.

A3 If you get married one day, I will play the violin.
If Sarah had read the book, she wouldn't have gone to see the movie.

If you met Brad Pitt, would you ask for an autograph?
If my mother hadn't broken her leg, she would have travelled to Italy.
I you read that travel guide, you would know a little more about California.

A4 Our school**, which** is located across a wonderful park**,** is old but beautiful.
It was my sister **who** gave me tickets for the rock concert.
The people I work with are very nice.
Last week I took my little niece to the cinema**, which** is just around the corner from where I live.

A5 It's not worth **buying** that book. It's boring.
My mother forced me **to study** some English vocabulary.
Dad permitted Hannah **to go** to the party on Saturday.
Would you mind **helping** me with the dishes?
I can hardly resist **eating** another ice cream.
Instead of **watching** TV, you had better go swimming!
Children usually love **to play / playing** games.
Cara was the best pupil **to play** the violin.

A6 Arriving at our friends' house, we were welcomed by their two little children.
Noticing that the old lady felt sick, Jim called an ambulance.
Not having worked in the garden for a while, my grandfather felt tired after mowing the lawn.
Having eaten too much chocolate, Mary felt awful.

A7 If I had more money, I would go shopping abroad more often.
It was wrong to send the children shopping on their own.
If you lived in Switzerland, you would have to go to school every afternoon.
My sister stopped smoking.
It's no use complaining about a bad teacher.
Jim wanted to know which team had won the match.
Sarah is used to practising the violin one hour a day.
I used to enjoy going to school. But since we've got a new principal, going to school is no longer any fun.

5 Wortschatz

Ü1

										1				
										D				
										I				
										S				
										C				
							2			U				
							S			S				
			4	F	A	C	T			S				
						7	A	T	T	I	T	U	D	E
5	S	U	B	J	E	C	T			O				
							E			N			3	
							M						P	
							E						R	
				6	C	O	N	C	L	U	S	I	O	N
							T						O	
													F	

Ü2

Zustimmung äußern	Ablehnung äußern	Meinungen erfragen
That's quite right.	I don't agree at all.	How do you feel / think about this?
That's my view exactly.	I don't think that's right.	What is your view on the matter?
I can't agree with you more.	I may be wrong but ...	Do you agree with that?
I agree (entirely).	That's not the way I see it.	Would you like to add anything?

Ü3 Today, German teenagers are allowed to take their driving test at the age of eighteen. However, a proposition has been made recently that 16-year-old teenagers should be able to take driving lessons so that they can take their driving test at the age of seventeen. As I'm going to be sixteen next month, this question is of great interest to me.
Many people think that 16-year-old-teenagers are not mature enough to drive. They are convinced that more accidents would happen if younger people were allowed to drive. On the one hand I must admit that they are partly right – not every 16-year-old really is mature enough. However, that can be true for older drivers, too: Some people might just never be mature enough to drive. For example, a lot of harm is done by people who drink and drive – alcohol makes driving dangerous, no matter how old someone is.

Furthermore, 16 year-olds are already allowed to take a driving test for motorcycles – which are much more dangerous than cars. Motorcycles only have two wheels, thus the driver needs a good sense of balance. In bad weather conditions, driving a motorcycle is dangerous because roads become slippery. Therefore, driving a car would be the better – and less dangerous – alternative. And on top of all that, public transport can be very lousy at the weekend and at night – a car could reduce young people's temptation to hitchhike, which is a big danger in itself. I'd like to finish by saying that I hope to be able to take my driving test soon!

Ü4 castle – lighthouse – pyramid – monastery → building
carrot – tomato – cucumber – lettuce → vegetable
bungalow – apartment building – semi-detached house – cottage → home
basketball – rugby – gymnastics – high jump → sports
drill – srewdriver – hammer – handsaw → tool
ball – doll – stuffed animal – marbles → toy

Ü5 **a)** unfortunate
b) violence
c) terrible
d) truth
e) clearence
f) inactive
g) health

Ü6 **a)** trustworthy
b) common
c) respectful
d) exercise

Ü7 girlfriend, greenhouse, beauty queen, candlelight, double-check, drugstore, everybody, eyewitness, swimming pool, breathtaking, homemade, pineapple, rocking horse *(Schaukelpferd)*, fireproof

Ü8 **a)** to visit
b) Adjektiv
c) airplane / plane
d) anybody, anyone, anything, anytime
e) access
f) slowly

Australia is a very large country with quite some people living in **remote** areas. Thus, modern infrastructure, especially health care **institutions,** hospitals etc., haven't been easily **accessible** for all of Australia's inhabitants und can still cause some problems. About a century ago, serious **illness** or accidents often meant death. The Australian inland holds many lonely **graves** of people who might have lived, had they been able to receive medical aid **quickly** enough. Therefore, in 1928, the RFDS was founded.
The service soon provided medical aid in emergencies and also a **comprehensive** primary health care to those living in the outback. Today, the RFDS is a very modern organization. **Aircraft** make about 80 % of the country accessible within two hours, and medical **advice** is provided via radio telephone at **any** time, day or night. And in cases of serious illness or accidents, emergency flights are made.
Until today, the RFDS is there to help the people – the people living in the outback as well as the many **visitors** and tourists travelling a wonderful continent!

Ü9 ordinary → gewöhnlich; ordinär → vulgar; personal → persönlich; Personal → staff; rent → die Miete; Rente → pension; receipt → Quittung; Rezept → prescription (Arztrezept) / recipe (Kochrezept); to wonder → sich fragen; sich wundern → to be surprised; chips → Pommes Frites; Chips → crisps

Ü10 Tim can't take any kind of ~~critic~~ → **criticism.** He always overreacts.
What's the ~~actual~~ → **current** score? – It's 2 : 3 for our team.
The ~~murder~~ → **murderer** could escape easily.
At the moment, I'm reading Harry Potter books. It's a very interesting ~~lecture~~ → **reading.**
The department store's ~~personal~~ → **staff** is taking a trip to the castle tomorrow.
Sarah has worked very hard this term, and indeed, her ~~notes~~ → **marks** have improved a lot.
Jeans are ~~hoses~~ → **trousers** that can be worn on many occasions.
Kate ~~wondered~~ → **was surprised** when Kevin told her about his problems.
die falsch verwendeten Begriffe und ihre Übersetzung: critic → Kritiker; actual → tatsächlich; murder → Mord; lecture → Vorlesung; personal → persönlich; notes → Notizen; hose → Feuerwehrschlauch; to wonder → sich fragen

Ü11 How much is the **rent** for this flat?
Your **criticism** of his work is not justified. He has done it quite well.
What's your **opinion** of the new film? – I didn't like it at all. I really don't understand why the **critic** has written such a positive article.

Can you tell me the **meaning** of that sign over there? – It tells you that you're not allowed to use your **mobile phone / cell phone.**
I really don't know why he doesn't talk to me anymore. **Perhaps** he is still angry because I didn't go out with him last weekend.
Most teenagers know exactly which **brand** of sneakers they want to wear.

Ü12 a) Everybody was happy to **accept** the invitation – everybody **except** Jamie who had rather gone to see the football match.
b) Some pupils dont like the new **principal** because she always judges according to very strict **principles.**
c) After living in a small apartment for five years, the Millers now **own** a house – but they **owe** quite some money to the bank, too.
d) Peter is a very good guitar player. He could be **self-confident,** but he has always been **self-conscious** about being red-haired.

Ü13 My grandfather only receives a small pension.
It is not very sensible to watch TV until three o'clock in the morning.
Have you ever donated to *Unicef*?
In addition to the monthly rent, the landlady asked for a deposit.
The current issue of this magazine reports on a big scandal.

Ü14 disgrace – dispiriting: disobedient – disgust – dishwasher – disk – ~~discuss~~
familiar – farm: farewell – fan club – family – ~~false~~ – far
horse – house: hot – ~~horror~~ – host – hour – hostility
keyboard – king: kill – kick – ~~key~~ – kind – kilo
life – light: lift – light – ~~lie~~ – lightning
ocean – off: odd – ~~occur~~ – odour – ocelot – of

Ü15 a) ['eksəsaɪz]
b) *verb* und *noun*
c) Das Wort *exercise* hat keine Pluralform, wenn es in der Bedeutung „Ausübung", „Bewegung" verwendet wird (Beispiel: *in the exercise of his duties – bei der Ausübung seiner Pflichten; A dog needs a lot of exercise. – Ein Hund braucht viel Bewegung.*) Wenn es sich aber um eine zählbare Aktion von Bewegungen handelt, wird ein *-s* angehängt, z. B. *stomach exercises – Bauchmuskelübungen*
d) wörtlich: *Leibesübung*, besser: *körperliche Betätigung*

Ü16

	Substantiv	Verb	Adjektiv
engl. dt.	acceptance **Annahme, Anerkennung**	to accept **annehmen, akzeptieren**	acceptable **annehmbar**
engl. dt.	ache **Schmerz**	**to ache** **wehtun, schmerzen**	**aching** **schmerzend**
engl. dt.	**deepness, depth** **Tiefe**	to deepen **vertiefen, verschärfen**	**deep** **tief**
engl. dt.	**study** **Studium**	**to study** **studieren, lernen**	studious **fleißig, eifrig**

Ü17 change → ['tʃeɪndʒ]
favour → ['feɪvə(r)]
words → [wɜːdz]
awful → ['ɔːfl]
bowl → [bəʊl]
apologize → [ə'polədʒaɪz]
result → [rɪ'zʌlt]

Ü18 a) oben rechts
b) Die Wendung *To whom it may concern* benutzt man in formellen Briefen, wenn man den Namen des Ansprechpartners nicht kennt („an die zuständige Abteilung").
c) 3 feet = 1 yard; 1 yard = 0,914 Meter
d) *ounce* ist eine Gewichtsangabe. *16 ounces* sind *1 pound,* das entspricht 0,454 kg.

Check-up Kapitel 5

A1 clear → **clarity, clearness**
real → **reality**
brilliant → **brilliance**
funny → **fun**
long → **length**

A2 comparison → **to compare**
quotation → **to quote**
harmony → **to harmonize**
height → **to heighten**
director → **to direct**
assistant → **to assist**

A3 If a doctor is convinced that some medicine might help, he writes a **prescription.**
The workers of a company are called **staff.**
If you are asking for a new job, the person who finally decides is called the **boss.**
Scientists usually work in a **laboratory.**

A4 to mention: to say (or to write) something without giving detailed information
to agree: to be of the same opinion
to propose: to suggest to do something
to persuade: to give good arguments in order to convince somebody
suggestion: an idea or a plan that one tells somebody else as a basis for discussion
attitude: the way one thinks and / or feels about something

A5 My sister is very good ~~in~~ **at** swimming.
She is very ~~timid~~ **anxious** to find a new job.
My brother's face was red ~~from~~ **with** anger when he came home from school.
I want proof ~~for~~ **of** your love. Give me a kiss now!
I'm sorry ~~for~~ **about** your bad test results.
We are late for the game. But I'm sure that somebody can tell us the ~~actual~~ **current** score.

A6

contradicting	agreeing	reacting to information
This does not appeal to me.	Yes, indeed.	I view that as ...
Sorry, but that's nonsense.	All right.	I my opinion, it's a good thing to ...
That's not the way I see it.	That's my view exactly.	We need a more balanced view.
I can't agree with you.	Definitely!	I wouldn't have thought ...

6 Stil

Ü1

formal words / phrases	informal equivalent
to encounter	to meet
gratified	glad
Would you please stop talking?	Quiet! / Shut up!
assistance	help
to menace	to threaten
We would like people to be quiet now.	Don't make a sound.
I couldn't agree more.	I'm with you there. / Right you are.
What I am trying to express is ...	I want to say ...
I am uncertain.	You're kidding. / I don't believe you.
I don't entirely disagree, but ...	I don't agree. / Oh, come on.
to elucidate	to make clear / to explain
to extinguish (a fire)	to put out

Ü2 to get cold feet → **to get scared (kalte Füße bekommen)**
to dawn on somebody → **to realize something for the first time (jdm. dämmern, bewusst werden)**
drivel → **silly nonsense (Blödsinn)**
to be for the birds → **to be worthless (für die Katz sein, nutzlos sein)**
He was struck dumb. → **He was speechless. (Er war wie vor den Kopf geschlagen, sprachlos)**

Ü3 Gesetzestext *(law text)*: **elevated**
offizielle Einladung *(letter of invitation)*: **stilted**
ein Leserbrief an eine Jugendzeitschrift *(a letter to the editor of a youth magazine)*: **colloquial**
Jugendliche im Gespräch untereinander *(youngsters among their peers)*: **slangy**
Flüche *(swear words)*: **vulgar**
politische Rede *(political speech)*: **elevated**
Lexikoneintrag *(entry in an encyclopaedia)*: **sophisticated**
Brief an ein Familienmitglied *(letter to a family member)*: **familiar**

Ü4 Lösungsvorschlag:
a) "Met that guy John yesterday. Wants to go and work in Australia. Has probably never been there."
b) "Yesterday I met Mr Smith, if you remember him, Sir. He used to work for our company. He has plans of embarking on a new life in Australia. Quite extraordinary, isn't it?"

Ü5 The cross is a **symbol** for Christianity.
The repeated use of a word or word group in order to emphasize an important aspect is called **repetition.**
A question which is not followed by an answer as the answer is obvious is called a **rhetorical question.**
a figure of speech implying an indirect comparison → **metaphor**
The repeated use of a syntactical structure in a sentence or in neighbouring sentences is called **parallelism.**
If the initial sounds are repeated at the beginning of or in the middle of neighbouring words for rhythmic effect, we talk of **alliteration.**

Ü6 You often earn less money than you expect.
The longer I stayed in London, the more I liked the city.
Although I don't have much money, I want to buy a bike.
He had better work harder.
London is worth visiting.
I bought a piece of cake for her to try.
If only I had a larger room.
I suggest having a party.
It doesn't matter how much he loves Pamela, she's not going to marry him.
It's the most boring book I've ever read.
It was such bad handwriting that I could not read the address.
I wish I could fly to the moon.

Ü7 that is to say → **sozusagen**
to lose heart → **den Mut verlieren**
to drop someone a line → **jemandem eine kurze Mitteilung schreiben**
to cut a long story short → **um es kurz zu machen / kurz und gut**
as the saying goes → **wie man so sagt**
the early bird catches the worm → **Morgenstund' hat Gold im Mund**
It's raining cats and dogs. → **Es regnet in Strömen.**

Ü8 Ich bin ganz Ohr. → **I'm all ears.**
eine Stecknadel fallen hören → **to hear a pin drop**
Ich habe ein Hühnchen mit dir zu rupfen. → **I've got a bone to pick with you.**
das Herz auf dem rechten Fleck haben → **to have the heart in the right place**
Halte mich auf dem Laufenden. → **Keep me posted!**

Ü9

interrupting an argument	agreeing with an argument	clarifying
Am I right in thinking …?	Very well!	What I meant was …
Please.	All right!	I'm not saying that. What I am saying is …
I beg your pardon?	Certainly.	I'm wondering if / whether …
Come on.	Of course!	Am I to understand …

Ü10 *Aleesha:* "Our trip to Holland was great, wasn't it? I really enjoyed it. Did you like it, too?"
Sarah: "I thought it was terrible. It was the weather that was the worst thing. It was pretty horrible. Because of the rain and the cold, I couldn't sleep at night. And I was really tired all day."
Aleesha: "Oh, I didn't think it was that bad."
Sarah: "What I also hated were Josh's speeches. They were totally unexciting."
Aleesha: "What did you think about the food?"
Sarah: "It was the food that was the worst thing. It just wasn't enough for me."
Aleesha: "Did you like anything at all?"
Sarah: "Well, I did enjoy being with Martin. He really told some good jokes."
Aleesha: "Well, at least you enjoyed one thing. However, I didn't like the fact that we had to go to bed at 10 p. m."
Sarah: "Right! Having to go to bed early made the trip even worse."
Aleesha: "So, I don't think I need to ask but will you still come with us next year?"
Sarah: "I don't think so. The trip was no fun at all."

Check-up Kapitel 6

A1 Don't we all love peace and hate war? → **rhetorical question**
"All the world's a stage …" *(William Shakespeare)* → **metaphor**
The dove is a **symbol** for peace.
New friends. New work. New life. → **parallelism**
It takes two to tango. → **alliteration**

A2 Thanks a lot. → Thank you very much.
to go to school → to attend school
to quit school → to leave school
Will you be quiet. → It could be quieter.
to take part in a discussion → to participate in a discussion
Can I use your car tomorrow? → May I use your car tomorrow?

A3 We must do everything to prevent Peter from drinking.
I suggest learning Italian.
The book is worth reading.
It didn't matter what he said, nobody listened to him.
The more I earn, the more money I spend.

A4 to draw the **shortest** straw → den Kürzeren ziehen
to hit the nail on the **head** → den Nagel auf den Kopf treffen
a drop in the **bucket** → ein Tropfen auf dem heißen Stein
as **dead** as a doornail → **mausetot**
to have **ants** in your pants → Hummeln im Hintern haben

A new **brush** sweeps clean. → Neue Besen kehren gut.
Let sleeping dogs **lie.** → Schlafende Hunde soll man nicht wecken.

A5 Lösungsvorschlag:
No politician **is always right.**
What I hate about **swimming** is that **one always gets wet.**
I didn't like **the museum.** I did like, however, **its cafeteria.**
Being lucky, **she survived the accident.**

A6 I suggest going for a walk.
Despite its heavy weight, the old man carried the suitcase upstairs himself.
We got up early so as not to miss our flight.
I will leave some money for you to buy yourself something for lunch.
I must do everything to prevent my girlfriend from taking drugs.
I wish I had visited my aunt one last time before her death.
Being ill, he could not come.

7 Umgang mit englischen Texten

Ü1 A Brutal Murder ... → **newspaper article**
A busy platform ... → **short story**
Scene I. A clearing ... → **play**
Globalization appears ... → **non-fictional text**
Earth has not anything ... → **poem (William Wordsworth, *Upon Westminster Bridge*)**
Whether I shall turn out to be ... → **novel (Charles Dickens, beginning of *David Copperfield*)**

Ü2 City Guide London → London is one of ...
A stairway to a better future → Here they are, a young couple from Mexico ...
Old schools, new methods → By encouraging the pupils ...
Keinen Text gibt es zu: A special occasion

Ü3 (nur lesen und Wörter nachschlagen)

Ü4 "Silicon Valley" is a non-fictional text about a region along the US-American West Coast. The text gives us information about the industrial development of that region and shows detailed background information on that development.

Ü5 **a)** Silicon Valley is located on the San Francisco, California, peninsula in the USA.
b) You could find vast orchards there.
c) It was concentrated on the East Coast.
d) It came from the wonderful sight in spring, when the valley was covered with blossoms of many colours.
e) He worked at Stanford University's department of electrical engineering near San Francisco.
f) The US Forces were interested in radio engineering for military reasons.
g) He advised them to start their own companies in the valley.
h) The company produces computers and electronic equipment.
i) You can find laboratories, new university departments, and factories.
j) It comes from the most important products produced there, the semiconductor chips, which are made of silicon.

Ü6 Lösungsvorschlag
a) Fred Terman was a professor of electrical engineering, working at Stanford University in California in the 1930s. He appears to have been a very ambitious man with own visions: He believed in the ideas and creativity of his students and not only encouraged them to start their own businesses, but offered real help and assistance by establishing new research departments. And although Fred Terman had fallen quite ill, he succeeded in realizing his plans. His vision became true, and today, Silicon Valley is one of the world centres of high technology.
b) Fruit orchards – pros:
- Trees are a more beautiful sight than laboratory buildings.
- Fruit orchards offer a number of blue collar jobs for the people.
- Fruit orchards are a good business because people always eat.

Fruit orchards – cons:
- Monocultures are prone to illnesses.
- Heavy weathers can easily destroy the crop and ruin the owners of an orchard.
- Orchards need a lot of water which is bad for the environment.

High Technology – pros:
- High Tech industry offers a number of white collar jobs.
- It's a future-oriented technology.

High Technology – cons:
- Concrete buildings ruin the landscape.
- Lots of jobs also mean lots of commuting traffic that pollutes the environment.

Ü7 A schoolgirl was praised for her honest act of handing in a bag with hundreds of pounds she had found in the street to the police in Canterbury, Kent, last week.
Harriet Walker, a nine-year old girl, was on her way to a local supermarket on Saturday, April 30, when she spotted the bag with the cash.

She said, "It was so strange. I almost fell over the bag. When my foot touched it, there was the noise of coins which were clinking inside. When I opened the bag there was lots of cash. I've never seen so much money ever before." Harriet rushed back to her family's home in Canterbury, Kent, where she and her dad counted the cash before they took it to the local police station. Harriet, a primary pupil at St Martin's Primary School, said, "I'm sure it must have been someone's pension or a whole week's wage. The poor person who lost the bag must be feeling so bad now."

Parents' pride

Mr Walker, 38, who is a freelance finance consultant, said: "It was Harriet's idea to hand it in to the police. She didn't want us to tell anybody about the bag with the cash. She's such a good girl. She's our pride." Harriet's mother, 37, a housewife, said: "She's always been absolutely honest. I'm so proud of her."

Sergeant William Smith from the police station said: "Anybody who detects a purse or bag with money shows honesty when he hands it in to the police. Unfortunately, not many people do so nowadays. Harriet is a good role model for other kids. Such an act of great honesty should be praised in public because it demonstrates how to be an upright citizen."

Details about the bag or where the money was found have not been disclosed. So the owner can prove that it is theirs.

Ü8 ***list of key phrases:***
- A schoolgirl was praised for her honest act of handing in a bag with hundreds of pounds she had found in the street to the police in Canterbury, Kent, last week.
- Harriet Walker, a nine-year old girl, was on her way to a local supermarket on Saturday, April 30, when she spotted the bag with the cash.
- ... she and her dad counted the money before they took it to the local police station.
- "She's our pride."
- "Harriet is a good role model for other kids."
- Details have not been disclosed.

main idea:
The newspaper tells the story of a 9-year-old who found a lot of money and handed it all in to the police. All the people involved – parents, police and journalists – praised her honesty.

Ü9 a) A schoolgirl was praised → A schoolgirl was applauded.
b) She spotted a bag → She saw a bag.
c) It was so strange. → It was so odd.
d) Harriet rushed back. → Harriet hurried back.
e) It was Harriet's idea to hand it in to the police. → It was Harriet's idea to take it to the police.
f) It demonstrates how to be ... → It shows how to be ...

Ü10 Lösungsvorschlag:
a) A little girl named Harriet Walker **was walking to** the local supermarket when she **suddenly saw** the bag with the cash.
b) Harriet **insisted that nobody else than the police should be informed** about the money bag.
c) Anybody who **finds / discovers** a purse or a bag with money **displays** honesty when he hands it in to the police.

Ü11 a) Harriet pities the poor person who lost the money because she can imagine how big a loss that must be.
b) Harriet's mother states that she is very pleased with her daughter.
c) The sergeant thinks Harriet must be seen as a perfect example for honest behaviour by everybody.

Ü12 The newspaper article written by Ken Parker and published in the Kentish Star on May 9th, 2006, tells the reader the story of a 9-year-old girl who found a lot of money on her way to the local supermarket.
To begin with, the author gives us details about how the girl found the money. The story is continued by telling the reader Harriet's reactions: how she ran home to her family, how she and her Dad counted the money, and that Harriet insisted on taking the money to the police. After that, the author informs us about the parent's reaction towards their kid's behaviour, that they both are very proud to have such an honest daughter. Furthermore, Police Sergeant William Smith is quoted as saying that such an act of honesty can't be applauded loud enough. The text concludes by saying that details about neither the bag nor the place where it was found should be published in order to give the proper owner a fair chance to prove his or her ownership.

Ü13 a) Dear Madam – ~~Hello Susan~~ – Gentlemen – Dear Dr. Roberts
b) Please inform us about ... – Thank you for your efforts in advance. ~~– Drop me a line.~~ – I should be pleased to receive your answer soon.
c) Yours faithfully – Sincerely yours – Yours sincerely – ~~Lots of love~~

■ **Ü14** Ich wäre Ihnen sehr verbunden, wenn Sie mir weitere Informationen zukommen lassen würden. → I would be grateful if you could send me further information.
Senden Sie uns bitte Einzelheiten über ... zu. → Please send us details concerning ...
Im Voraus vielen Dank für Ihre Mühe. → Thank you for your efforts in advance.
Mit Bezug auf Ihr Inserat in ... → With reference to your advertisement in ...
Die am 11. Februar bestellten Produkte sind noch nicht bei uns eingegangen. → We have not yet received the items ordered on 11th February.

■ **Ü15** Dear **Sir or Madam,**
I am writing **to express** my dissatisfaction with the poor service provided by The Railroad Company.
I am a teacher working at a Canterbury comprehensive school. Yesterday, I took my A-level students on a trip to London, **travelling on** the 8.10 train from Canterbury to London. Not only was the train thirty minutes late leaving Canterbury, but we **were further delayed** at the outskirts of London for no apparent reason. No information or **apology** was offered and I still do not know the reason for our delay.
In addition / Furthermore, as one of my students fell sick, I asked a member of the staff to bring us a glass of water. Your staff member was most **unhelpful / unsympathetic,** telling me to go and get a glass of water myself.
Moreover, the many delays and troubles caused us to miss our tour guide who **was supposed** to meet our group at Euston Station. I had to show my students around London on my own, **missing out** on the many interesting comments a professional guide can offer.
I am deeply convinced that you will appreciate that this level of service is **unacceptable.** Thus, I expect **to receive** compensation for all the inconveniences and look forward to a full **explanation.**
Yours **faithfully / sincerely** ...

■ **Ü16** Unfortunately, Sarah has made many mistakes: The language she uses is too informal, the information she gives about herself is not the type of information a possible employer wants to have, and on top of all that, she has made a couple of formal mistakes: Sarah doesn't give her full address and she forgot to date her letter. Furthermore, the paper she looked in to find the advertisement was not a current one, so the job might be taken already. Besides all that, she doesn't give any reason why she qualifies as an au pair.

■ **Ü17**

Lisa Sommerfeldt
Königstraße 34
80230 München
Tel: 0049 – 89 – 9 87 65 43 21

24th March, 2006

Mr and Mrs Smith
33 Main Street
London W24 5LU

Application for the post of au pair

Dear Mr and Mrs Smith,
With reference to your advertisement in yesterday's edition of our local newspaper "Münchner Nachrichten", I would like to apply for the post of au pair with you.
At the moment, I am attending year 10 of the Isar-Realschule here in Munich and have been studying English as a foreign language for six years now. Furthermore, the type of school I still attend teaches home economics, and I have been learning cooking and housekeeping for four years now. I expect to finish school in July.
I would be delighted to be able to work as an au pair with your family from August 1st.
I have one 12-year-old brother as well as 9-year-old twin sisters whom I regularly take care of because our parents both work. My father works as a manager for a well-known car company, and my mother works part-time in a bank. Furthermore, the school I still attend offers home economics, too – a field in which I have taken several classes; I am able to prepare proper meals and I can keep a household tidy.
I would enjoy looking after your children and at the same time getting to know the British way of life, which I find very interesting and attractive.
I am looking forward to hearing from you soon.

Yours sincerely,
Lisa Sommerfeldt

Check-up Kapitel 7

■ **A1** The end of a piece of writing is called **ending** or **conclusion.**
A person in a piece of writing, a play or a movie is a **character.**
The place where something happens is the **setting.**
The most important statement in a text can be called the **main idea.**

An (invented) description of events and / or people is called a **story.**

A2 report – newspaper article – official invitation – ~~novel~~
letter of complaint – letter of enquiry – ~~love letter~~ – letter of application
short story – novel – poem – ~~election speech~~

A3 Lösungsvorschlag:
The text describes the economic situation in modern Ireland. The country used to be dominated by agriculture and is an industrial country today (most important: computer and software industry).
Furthermore, the text informs its readers about tourism and the service industry in Ireland. A lot of international companies maintain big businesses in Ireland due to young and well-trained workers.
The text concludes by saying that Ireland, once a poor country, is now on the same level as its neighbours regarding its economy.

A4

letter of enquiry	letter of complaint	letter of application
We have read about your product in the press.	On top of all this ...	I am writing in response to your advertisement for a ... in today's edition of ...
We have seen from your brochure / catalogue that ...	As a consequence ...	With reference to your advertisement in ...
I would appreciate if you could send me further information on / about ...	I was disappointed to find out that ...	I have some experience in ...
It would also be helpful to know ...	Please replace the items as soon as possible.	I am currently studying ...
Please let me know ...	I expect compensation for ...	Please find enclosed a copy of ...
I would be interested to know ...	I eagerly await your comments.	I am available for an interview any time.
Would you please send me details of ...	I would like a full refund.	I am looking forward to hearing from you.

A5 Lösungsvorschlag:
Dear Sir or Madam,
This is an application to undertake a period of work experience at your headquarters in New York.
At present, I am a pupil at the Humboldt Gymnasium in Munich, attending year 12. After my A-levels I plan to study mechanical engineering and would thus like to collect some on-the-job experiences in that field.
By working in an English speaking country, I furthermore intend to improve my language skills.
I would be very grateful if you would offer me an opportunity for work experience from August 1st to August 31st, 2007.
Thank you in advance for taking the trouble to read my application.

Yours sincerely, ...

Enclosures: CV
Certified copies of reports

8 Englisch als Weltsprache

Ü1 petrol → **gas**
autumn → **fall**
mark → **grade**
chemist's → **drugstore**
lift → **elevator**
headmaster → **principal**
lorry → **truck**
tap → **faucet**
pavement → **sidewalk**

Ü2 neighbour → **neighbor**
flavour → **flavor**
to colonialise → **to colonialize**
harbour → **harbor**
monologue → **monolog**
honour → **honor**
metre → **meter**
programme → **program**
organisation → **organization**

Ü3 Dear Linda,
Once again, I'd like to thank you again for the wonderful time with you and your family in Michigan. I really had a wonderful time! However, I had to acknowledge the fact the English we speak at home is different from your language. When I told my Mum that we went on a walk with your little brother in his **stroller (BE: pushchair – Kinderwagen)** and that we bought him some **candy (BE: sweets – Süßigkeiten)**, she asked twice what we did to little Jamie! She had also never heard about **diapers (BE: nappies – Windeln)** and **pacifiers (BE: dummies – Schnuller)** before! On the other hand, Mum was surprised to hear that **private schools (BE: public schools – Privatschule)** are common in the States, too.

Do you remember the colorful **pantyhose (BE: colourful tights – bunte Strumpfhosen)** I bought? My friend Susan complimented me about them. Susan also really liked the **purse (BE: handbag – Handtasche)** I bought for her as a **gift (BE: present – Geschenk)** – as I had suspected, she went crazy for its deep green **color (BE: colour – Farbe)**!
Talking about friends, I especially liked the weekend we spent together with your friends staying overnight in your **RV (BE: camper – Wohnmobil)**. **Vacations (BE: holidays – Ferien)** have never been so much fun for me before!
And now I'm looking forward to the summer, when you'll come over to London! I hope you'll like it here as much as I liked it with you.
Take care,
Mary-Lou

Ü4 Lösungsvorschläge:
Payback Card, Hype, Performance, Milkshake, Walkman, Butler

Ü5 Lösungsvorschläge:
Kosmetik: Make-up, Showergel, Lipgloss, Aftershave, Bodylotion
Musik: DJ, CD-Player, Rock'n'Roll, Soundcheck
Geschäftswelt: Business, prepaid, Recycling, Human Resources
Kultur und Medien: Photoshooting, Cartoon, Movie, Public viewing, Display
Verkehr: Park-and-ride, Rushhour, Airbus

Ü6 Im Musikbusiness werden neue Bands oft dadurch bekannt, dass sie einen Sampler zusammenstellen, auf dem sich ihr Hit befindet. Bands, die den Durchbruch schaffen, benötigen dann meist einen Manager.
Um ihr Album zu promoten, geht die Band auch auf Tour und spielt live. Bevor der Gig onstage beginnen kann, ist ein Soundcheck erforderlich. Danach ziehen sich die Bandmitglieder meist in den Backstage-Bereich zurück, wo ihnen Dressingrooms und Catering zur Verfügung stehen. Fans haben zu diesem Bereich in der Regel keinen Zutritt, es sei denn, sie haben gute Connections und standen beim Einlass auf der VIP-Liste.
Musikbusiness → Musikgeschäft
Band → Musikgruppe
Hit → Musikstück, das zum Verkaufsschlager geworden ist
Manager → Führungskraft, leitende Persönlichkeit, *auch* Betreuer
promoten → Werbung machen
live → „live", nicht vom Band
Gig → Auftritt
onstage → auf der Bühne
Soundcheck → das Ausprobieren der Akustik unter den jeweiligen Bedingungen; Klangprobe
Backstage → hinter der Bühne, hinter den Kulissen
Dressingrooms → Garderobe
Catering → Verpflegung
Fans → Anhänger
Connections → Beziehungen
VIP-Liste → Gästeliste

Check-up Kapitel 8

A1

AE	BE	deutsche Bedeutung
chips	crisps	Chips
cookie	biscuit	Keks
movie	film	Kinofilm
notebook	exercise book	Übungsheft
robe	dressing gown	Morgenmantel
subway	underground	U-Bahn
toll-free	free of charge	gebührenfrei
trash	rubbish	Abfall

A2 *the Bush administration:* Die korrekte Übersetzung lautet: *die Regierung Bush.* Der Begriff *the ... adminstration* meint immer den Präsidenten und sein Team!
it doesn't make sense: Die korrekte Übersetzung lautet: *Es ergibt keinen Sinn / es ist sinnlos.*
handyman: Das Wort hat nichts mit Handys zu tun. Gemeint ist ein Bastler / Heimwerker.
in 2007: Im Deutschen braucht man vor Jahreszahlen kein *in:* Es heißt z. B.: *2007 stiegen die Zinsen erneut.*
Make a difference bedeutet *Mach einen Unterschied*, im Sinne von „mach es andere als andere, handle klüger".

A3 Public Relations → Öffentlichkeitsarbeit
canceln → absagen, rückgängig machen
Snack → Zwischenmahlzeit
Casting → Rollenbesetzung
Shootingstar → Person oder Sache, die schnell an die Spitze gelangt; Senkrechtstarter

Feedback → Rückmeldung
Meeting → Konferenz, Treffen
Website → Webseite *(nur 1:1-Übersetzung möglich)*
Callcenter → Büro für telefonische Dienstleistungen

■ **A4** *Jeff*: "Here are your travel vouchers: your plane tickets, some hotel addresses and – very important – some immigration forms. Please note that you've got to fill out these forms before you clear customs."
Mrs Green: "So we've got to **fill in** some forms? Well, we'll manage."
Jeff: "As soon as you've arrived at the airport, transportation to your hotel is really easy. Take a shuttle from the airport to the hotel, hand your baggage to the bellboy and check in at the reception."
Mr Green: "You mean we shall hand our **luggage** to the **porter?** Never! I don't trust anybody than myself!"
Jeff: "Oh, I'm sorry. You don't have to do that. But it would make things easier for you."
Mrs Green: "We are not that old!"
Jeff: "And as a little gift from the travel agency, here are two daypacks with the company logo. Have a wonderful vacation!"
Mr Green: "Well, we've never used **rucksacks** before. But thank you very much for the **present.** We are really excited and we are looking forward to our **holiday.**"

Das 3-fach-Prinzip für bessere Noten

Die neue Lernhilfenreihe „Einfach klasse in" für die 5. bis 10. Klasse überzeugt durch ihren besonderen Aufbau:

- Übersichtlich strukturiert in die drei Lernbausteine **Wissen – Üben – Testen**
- Alle wichtigen Lernbereiche einer Klassenstufe in einem Band zusammengefasst
- Mit persönlichem Klassenarbeitsplaner
- Nach den neuesten Bildungsplänen der Bundesländer entwickelt

DEUTSCH

Einfach klasse in
Deutsch 5. Klasse
ISBN 978-3-411-72151-1

Einfach klasse in
Deutsch 6. Klasse
ISBN 978-3-411-72161-0

Einfach klasse in
Deutsch 7. Klasse
ISBN 978-3-411-72251-8

Einfach klasse in
Deutsch 8. Klasse
ISBN 978-3-411-72261-7

Einfach klasse in
Deutsch 9. Klasse
ISBN 978-3-411-72411-6

Einfach klasse in
Deutsch 10. Klasse
ISBN 978-3-411-72421-5

ENGLISCH

Einfach klasse in
Englisch 5. Klasse
ISBN 978-3-411-72131-3

Einfach klasse in
Englisch 6. Klasse
ISBN 978-3-411-72141-2

Einfach klasse in
Englisch 7. Klasse
ISBN 978-3-411-72271-6

Einfach klasse in
Englisch 8. Klasse
ISBN 978-3-411-72281-5

Einfach klasse in
Englisch 9. Klasse
ISBN 978-3-411-72591-5

Einfach klasse in
Englisch 10. Klasse
ISBN 978-3-411-72601-1

MATHEMATIK

Einfach klasse in
Mathematik 5. Klasse
ISBN 978-3-411-72171-9

Einfach klasse in
Mathematik 6. Klasse
ISBN 978-3-411-72181-8

Einfach klasse in
Mathematik 7. Klasse
ISBN 978-3-411-72431-4

Einfach klasse in
Mathematik 8. Klasse
ISBN 978-3-411-72441-3

Einfach klasse in
Mathematik 9. Klasse
ISBN 978-3-411-72571-7

Einfach klasse in
Mathematik 10. Klasse
ISBN 978-3-411-72581-6

Jeder Band:
128 Seiten. Kartoniert, mit Umschlagklappen

Weitere Fächer in Vorbereitung

Stichwortfinder